Own It!
Real Estate
Dictionary

William E Keeler

ISBN:1503070344
ISBN-13:9781503070349

DEDICATION

In loving Memory of my brother,
Steven T. Keeler

January 8th, 1966 - August 28th, 2010

CONTENTS

0 -A

1099 - An IRS-designated form used by businesses to report payments to consultants or service providers who are paid on a contractual basis. A copy of the 1099 is provided to the contractor for preparing income taxes and documenting gross income. Mortgage lenders will sometimes review a borrower's 1099, if any to confirm tax return figures.

A-Credit - An informal term referring to borrowers and applicants with very good credit history; they usually have credit scores of 650+, with A-plus credit starting at 720. Conforming loan programs require A-credit of its applicants. In the mortgage industry, A-credit borrowers must satisfy all of the following requirements: (1) no foreclosure or bankruptcy within the past seven years; (2) no late payments on their mortgage history during the past year and no more than one late payment in the past two years; (3) no more than one late payment on any installment loan during the past year and no more than two during the past two years; (4) no more than two late payments on revolving accounts during the past year and no more than four during the past two years; (5) no open collection accounts; and (6) a credit score of at least 650.

A-Frame Roof - A type of gable roof with high, steep (chalet-like) roofs. It is ideal for areas with high snowfall, as it allows gravity to prevent dangerous build-up.

Abandonment - The surrender of a property's ownership without a formal or legal successor. Abandonment can apply to either fee simple or leasehold properties. Landlords must follow local laws when trying to reclaim rental units abandoned by the tenant.

Absentee Owner - An owner of real estate property who does not manage or reside at the subject property.

Absorption Cooling System - A method of air cooling that begins by boiling a water and lithium bromide solution (the absorbent). The steam goes through a separator, which takes away the lithium bromide and sends it back to the absorber. The steam, however, continues on to a condenser, where it turns back into water. That water then flows into an evaporator, where it is turned into a very cold water vapor (the refrigerant). This refrigerant is then pumped through coils in the furnace where it cools the air or water that is then used to cool rooms.

Absorption Rate - The period required to lease a property.

Abstract of Title - The summary history of the documents affecting the title to a real estate property, documenting its conveyances and encumbrances.

Abstract of Title with Attorney's Opinion - A type of evidence of title that begins with the compilation of a title abstract, followed by an attorney's review and written opinion of the status and marketability of title. This opinion is not a guarantee, but a legal opinion that is often sufficient to perfecting title.

Accelerated Cost Recovery System - A method of depreciation introduced by the Economic Recovery Act of 1981. It calculates the useful life of various property types, for the purpose of determining depreciation.

Accelerated Depreciation - A faster method of depreciation than the straight-line method.

Acceleration Clause - The clause in a mortgage, or deed of trust, that allows the lender to "accelerate" the payment schedule—demanding immediate payment of the loan principal. Standard residential mortgage loans do not allow unrestricted acceleration clauses; this clause is normally used by the lender to demand the entire balance due immediately if the borrower fails to meet loan obligations (i.e., default).

Access Right - The legal right of entrance or exit to a real estate property. American real estate laws prohibits properties from being landlocked and requires easements through neighboring properties to provide access to landlocked properties.

Accession - Real estate term referring to the legal process by which trade fixtures permanently become part of the real property, usually when the fixture is not removed by a departing tenant.

Accretion - The gradual addition of land by force of nature. For example, tidal forces may shift sand from one coastline to an inlet several miles down. The inlet is experiencing accretion.

Accrual Basis - An accounting method that records expense and income amounts as soon as they are incurred--regardless of whether funds have been disbursed or collected. Compare with the Cash Basis entry.

Accrued Depreciation, Accumulated Depreciation - The total of depreciation that has been claimed on a property. Owners of investment real estate must claim depreciation deductions on their annual tax returns for the investment property. When the property is sold, the accrued depreciation deductions must be reclaimed and taxes must be paid on the accrued depreciation .

Accrued (Closing) Expenses - Those expenses payable at closing that have been accumulated but not yet paid by the seller. For example, real estate taxes that are paid in arrears must be prorated to debit the seller for unpaid accrued taxes.

Accrued Interest - Unpaid but due interest payments on a loan.

Acknowledgment - With deeds, the acknowledgment is a witnessing declaration verifying the validity of the grantor's signature. F

Acquisition Cost - Charges and expenses related to a real estate purchase, over and above the property's price. These expenses will include title insurance , credit checks, property appraisals and legal fees. This is usually called the "closing" or "settlement" costs.

Acre - The traditional measurement of land size consisting of 43,560 square feet or 4,840 square yards. Farm land, unimproved land and residential properties are often indicated in acres.

Active Income - Revenue or income generated from a person's direct effort or investor's active participation in a business' operations. Salary and wages from regular employment or self-employment are primary examples of active income. This label comes into play in discussions about Tax Shelters, which contrasts active income with portfolio and passive income, which are the three types of ordinary income.

Actual Cash Value - The type of coverage reimbursement provided by standard property insurance policies. This value is based on the original cost of the subject property minus depreciation. Compare with full replacement coverage.

Actual Eviction - A legal remedy available to landlords who have lessees in holdover tenancy. Actual eviction requires the landlord to decline all attempted rent payments, give the holdover tenant adequate notice and filing for court action to forcibly remove the holdover tenant. Federal, state and local consumer protection laws normally require landlords to follow strict guidelines when trying to evict tenants. In most cases, the eviction process can take several months as the eviction must be approved by the local courts and enforced by the sheriff's office.

Actual Notice - Legal term referring to information that a person or party has received through reading, seeing or hearing. Compare with Constructive Notice entry.

Ad valorem tax - A standard term for the real estate tax of a specific parcel of property. As the name suggests, this tax is based on the valuation of the property. The traditional method for calculating a parcel's property tax assessment is to multiply the assessed value—after any adjustments or deductions for homestead owners, senior citizens, etc.—by the official tax "millage" rate and any equalizer rate..

Addendum - An addition to a note, deed or other legal document that amends or clarifies the terms of the original document.

Adjustable Rate Mortgage (ARM) - A type of mortgage financing that allows the lender to periodically make interest rate adjustments, with consequent payment recalculation. The adjustments are according to an independent market index, such as U.S. Treasury Bill yields or the Federal Reserve's Cost of Funds Index (COFI). Adjustments are normally made once each period, at the anniversary of the loan; for example, a 2-year ARM adjusts its interest rates every two years. The primary exception is ARM loans based on the Prime rate, which are adjusted sporadically by major banks.

Adjusted Gross Income (AGI) - With tax returns, this is the consumer's taxable income after all deductions, carry-overs and adjustments have been included. Mortgage lenders do not use this amount for their gross qualifying income calculation. However, mortgage lenders do often include the AGI in its qualifying income calculation for self-employed applicant.

Adjusted Tax Basis - Also called, adjusted cost basis, this is the net book value of a property, on which a capital gain or loss is based. This calculation begins with the basis (original purchase price), to which capital improvements made since the purchase and buying expenses are added; any depreciation taken for tax-related deductions is then subtracted from that amount to arrive at the adjusted tax basis. When the property is sold, the capital gains tax is calculated as the new sales price minus the tax basis.

Adjustment Interval - On an adjustable rate mortgage (ARM) loan, the time between changes in the interest rate and/or monthly payment— typically ranging from six months and one year to ten years, depending on the specific program selected.

Administrator - A court-appointed individual for the purpose of directing and eventually disposing of the property of a person who has died without a will.

Administrator's Deed - A deed that conveys to a purchaser the real estate property of an individual who has died intestate (without a will).

Adverse Possession - Similar to squatter rights, adverse possession is a statute of limitation that bars the true owner from asserting his claim to a real estate property. However, this is only applicable if that owner has not made any notices or actions to stop the adverse occupant during the proscribed statutory period. Typical statutory periods are seven to thirty years. As long as the true owner makes a notice to the occupant at least once during the statutory period, the statutory term begins anew. This should not be confused with involuntary alienation, which is more of an active legal maneuver.

After-Tax Cash Flow - The income funds remaining after all operating expenses, including taxes, are paid.

After-Tax Rate - The rate of return calculation based on the after-tax income divided by the equity.

Agency - A legal relationship between a principal and an agent arising from a contract in which the principal engages the agent to perform certain acts on the principal's behalf. Agencies are typically created in one of four ways: expressed agency, implied agency, agency by estoppel and agency by necessity.

Agency By Estoppel - A type of agency relationship created when a principal, through statements or actions, leads a third party to believe that someone is his or her agent--and that third party relies on it. Even if no previous agency relationship existed, that someone is now an agent for the principal in the context of this third party.

Agency By Necessity - A type of agency relationship created in an emergency situation, when it may be unnecessary to obtain the principal's consent to expand or create an agency.

Agency Guidelines - In the mortgage industry, Fannie Mae, Freddie Mac and Ginnie Mae are considered agencies because they were established by the government to develop the secondary mortgage market.

Agreement of Sale - Known by various names, such as contract of purchase, purchase agreement, or sales agreement according to location or jurisdiction. A contract in which a seller agrees to sell and a buyer agrees to buy, under certain specific terms and conditions spelled out in writing and signed by both parties.

Air Rights - Property right providing for legal ownership of space above a parcel of land or within a building. For example, developers may negotiate for control air rights above urban railways and then construct buildings above these railways. The most common application of air rights are condominiums: in most cases, unit owners only own the air space within the unit walls.

Alienation Clause - Also called a due-on-sale clause, this is an element in mortgage deeds that allows the lender to demand full repayment of the current principal balance if the title is ever transferred or substantially altered, without prior consent from the lender. Essentially, this is a provision to prohibit loan assumptions and title assignments.

Alienation of Property - A legal term describing the transfer of property from the current owner. Such alienation can either be voluntary (as in the case of a lease) or involuntary.

B

B-Credit - An informal term referring to borrowers and applicants with several recent minor delinquencies or credit problems; they usually have credit scores between 580 to 650. Conforming programs tend to deny B-credit applicants. However, B-credit applicants usually have a good chance of improving to A-credit in a relatively short period of one to two years. In the mortgage industry, B-credit borrowers normally have one or more of the following traits: (1) no bankruptcies or foreclosures in the past five years and no repossessions or major judgments in the past four years; (2) three to six late payments on mortgage and installment debts during the past two years; (3) five to eight late payments on revolving debts in the past two years; (4) unpaid collections of $500 to $10,000. Note that a borrower with no recorded credit history is normally graded B.

Back-End Ratio - When qualifying the applicant's income, the back-end ratio is the total debt-to-income (DTI) ratio limit that deals with all long-term liabilities. Unlike the front-end ratio that considers only the housing expense qualification—which is also considered long-term—the back-end ratio includes all other long-term debts, as well as the housing expense. The conforming loan limit for the back-end ratio is usually 33% to 38%, which means that the sum total of all long-term monthly payments (including total housing expenses) should not exceed 33% to 38% of the borrower's gross income, depending on the specific loan program. Thus, if you add together the monthly payments on all your loans, credit cards and projected housing expenses, then divide by your gross monthly income, you will arrive at your projected back-end ratio. However, certain nonconforming programs allow back-end ratios in excess of 55%.

Back-Up Contract - A real estate purchase agreement that becomes effective only if a primary contract with another party fails to close. The buyer in the back-up contract understands that he or she may not be able to purchase the property, particularly if the primary buyer is able to complete a purchase.

Backfill - The gravel, soil or other material replaced in the space around a building wall after the foundation and external subterranean walls have been set.

Bad Debt Allowance - Accounting terminology used in real estate that enters a reduction allowance against the gross income of an investment. The bad debt allowance assumes that certain invoices or payable rent will never be collected.

Balance Sheet - A financial statement that calculates an entity's assets, liabilities and equity for a defined period. The balance sheet normally displays the equity amount as equaling the total of asset and liability entries.

Balloon Frame - The basic method used with many homes, in which light wood beams (joists) were nailed to supports (studs) to form a framework for exterior and interior finishing. This framing style was a by-product of the industrial revolution which was able to mass-produce necessary building material to meet growing housing needs. The key element of the balloon frame is the web of lighter materials.

Balloon Loan - A type of loan whose term is less than the length of the amortization. It is usually a short-term fixed-rate loan which involves small payments for a certain period of time and one large payment for the remaining amount of the principal at a time specified in the contract. For example, a 5-year balloon is one in which the loan matures in 5 years but is amortized for 30 years. [Translation: the monthly payments are calculated for a 30-year pay-back period (so they're lower); but after five years, the loan term expires and the borrower must repay or refinance the entire remaining balance.] The balloon loan interest rate and monthly payments are lower than standard fixed-rate loans, but the entire principal balance is due at the end of the term—hence a large balloon payment. The most typical balloon loans are 5-year and 7-year balloons, although 10-year and 15-year balloons are also available.

Baluster - Small posts or vertical ornaments between stairs and their bannister.

Bankruptcy - The formal court order that provides protection to debtors so as to allow them to reorganize their finances. U.S. bankruptcy laws provide many consumers with a method to reestablish their financial health, without being completely drained by creditors. There are primarily two types of personal bankruptcy options: chapter 13 and chapter 7. Chapter 13 essentially reorganizes the consumer's debts, while the chapter 7 eliminates debts after liquidation of available assets. However, a bankruptcy will have a severe impact on the applicant's financing efforts for a period of five to ten years.

Bank Statement - The periodic itemization of transactions that is provided by depository institutions to its clients. Many lenders will request copies of the applicant's bank statements to document existence and source of sufficient funds, as well as to provide an alternative method for documenting income. [With "limited documentation" loan program, the applicant can use the average monthly deposits for the past 12 months as his or her qualifying income.]

Bannister - Hand rails for stairs.

Bargain and Sale Deed - A type of deed that offers the grantee no expressed guarantees against encumbrances, unless specifically stated. However, a covenant of seisin is normally assumed.

Base Line - A real estate surveying term used with the rectangular survey system, base lines refer to identified lines running east-to-west across the nation, from which specific parcels of property are measured. Base lines are normally used in conjunction with range lines, principal meridians, township lines, townships and sections.

Base Molding, Baseboard - Construction term referring to trim-work placed along the bottom of a wall, effectively covering the wall-floor corner.

Base Rent - The minimum rent due under a lease agreement that requires additional assessments based on the property's operating expenses. Triple-Net lease arrangements, for example, charges the tenant a base rent plus additional assessments for the tenant's share of taxes, insurance premiums and operating expenses.

Basecoat - When plaster is used, the first coat of plaster is often used to set a base. The second coat is called a brown coat.

Basis - The owner's basis is the initial cost of the property. However, when calculating potential capital gain taxes, the property owner must apply the adjusted tax basis--which takes into account other capital improvements, purchase costs and depreciations taken.

Basis Point - A calculation of 1/100 of one percent. A point is calculated as one percent of a gross amount. A basis point is 1/100th of that point.

Batten - Any strip of wood used to cover a joint. Most often, it is a narrow piece of board used to cover the vertical joints of plywood siding.

Batter Board - Horizontal boards used to mark a building's layout prior to construction.

Bay - The unfinished area or space between a row of columns and the bearing wall.

Bay Window - A type of window that projects from the side wall of a house or structure. Typical bay windows actually consists of three windows: the central one is parallel to the wall, while the side windows angle from the side of the central window to the wall. Bay windows can provide more light and ventilation than standard configurations, as well as add space to a room.

Bay Depth - The distance from the corridor wall to the real window or wall.

Bead - A narrow, rounded type of trim molding.

Beam - A horizontal load-supporting length of wood, metal or other very strong material.

Bearing Wall - A wall that supports a floor or roof of a building.

Before-Tax Cash Flow - The income or revenue available after operating expenses, but before the payment of any taxes. Compare to the After-Tax Cash Flow entry.

Benchmark - A real estate surveying term referring to the bronze markers used by the U.S. Coast Guard & Geodetic Survey to indicate sea level measurement at various points in the country. Surveyors can use these benchmarks as local datum from which to measure elevation.

Beneficiary - Essentially, the beneficiary is the person or party who will benefit from a particular agreement or deed. With trusts, the beneficiary is the person or party who benefits from the trust.

C

C-Credit - An informal term referring to borrowers and applicants with damaged and poor credit. C-grade consumers are usually delinquent on several accounts, and demonstrate an inability to efficiently manage debt; they usually have credit scores obetween 500 to 579. For most C-grade consumers, their only financing hope would be with non-conforming loan programs. In the mortgage industry, C-credit borrowers usually have one or more of the following traits: (1) a bankruptcy, foreclosure or repossession during the past two to three years; (2) at least 60-90 days behind on mortgage or large installment debts ; (3) at least nine late payments on revolving accounts in the past two years; and (4) more than one open collection account. However, with proper attention to debt payments, a C-credit borrower can usually return to A-grade within two to three years.

Calendar Year - The 12-month period beginning January 1 and ending December 31.

Call Provision - Similar to the acceleration clause, this clause in certain mortgage documents allows the lender to accelerate the debt payments. However, the call provision is conditioned on certain events--unlike the acceleration clause, which is activated only by default.

Canceled Check - A check used for payment that has been processed through the issuer's bank and returned to the issuing payer. The canceled check will normally have processing ink-stamps on its back and can be used as proof of payment.

Cant - A slanting roof board used to eliminate sharp right angles.

Cantilever - A beam that is fixed on one end but is left free floating on the other end. This is sometimes used for roofs andoverhanging porches.

Cap (Interest) - The maximum adjustment that a lender may make to the interest rate of an Adjustable Rate Mortgage (ARM) loan. There are mainly two types of interest rate caps: periodic and lifetime. The periodic cap limits rate adjustments from one period to the next, while the lifetime cap limits the maximum interest rate to which the loan may rise throughout the entire life of the loan.

Cap (Payment) - The maximum adjustment that a lender may make to the monthly payment of an Adjustable Rate Mortgage (ARM) loan. The payment cap limits periodic adjustments to the monthly loan payment, regardless of any interest rate adjustment. Note, however, that ARM loans with payment caps often produce negative amortization, wherein the principal increases instead of decreases.

Cap (Principal)

D

D-Credit - An informal term referring to borrowers and applicants with extremely damaged and abysmal credit, usually with credit scores below 500. The only financing hope for D-credit borrowers would be expensive non-conforming loan programs. D-grade borrowers are often currently in foreclosure , bankruptcy or repossession—or have just completed such actions within the past year. Consumers can still be graded "D" when the foreclosure , bankruptcy or repossession is two to five years old if that consumer has not made strides in rebuilding credit. However, with proper attention to debt payments, a D-credit borrower can usually return to A-grade within five to seven years.

Daily Interest - The current interest charge for each day. The daily interest is used with prepaid expenses and per diem assessments. Interest rates are normally indicated as annual rates. The daily interest rate is usually calculated as the current principal balance times the annual rate, divided by 365 days.

Damper - The hinged lid in a fireplace flue that controls the draft coming in and out of the fireplace. The damper is kept closed when the fireplace is not being used.

Datum - A real estate surveying term referring to the level surface from which elevations are measured. Every large city has a datum, although most surveyors use the U.S. Coast Guard & Geodetic Survey datum.

De Minimus PUD (Planned Unit Development) - A planned unit development (PUD) that has a relatively minimal amount of common property and improvements.

Debt - The borrower's obligation to repay a lender. It is sometimes referred to as liabilities.

Debt Service - The regular payment amount required by a loan debt. With most mortgage loans, the debt service refers to the monthly or annual P&I payment.

Debt Service Ratio - Also called the "debt coverage ratio," the DSR is the a measurement of a property's ability to handle a loan debt. The DSR is the projected debt service payments divided by the after-tax net operating income. Commercial lenders often impose minimum DSR restrictions of 1.10 to 1.35. The most common DSR is 1.2, which means that lenders require the property to produce net operating income that is at least 120% higher than the projected debt service payments.

Debt-To-Income (DTI) Ratio - The primary method used by lenders to qualify prospective borrowers for mortgage financing. The DTI ratio is basically the total monthly debt payments divided by the gross monthly income. Two types of income ratios are normally considered by most lenders: the front-end (housing) ratio and the back-end (total debt) ratio. The housing ratio is the projected housing payment divided by the gross monthly income; the total debt ratio is the projected housing payment plus all other long-term debt payments, divided by the gross monthly income.

Declaration of Condominium - Sometimes called a master deed, this document provides basic information about the community's land, structures, buildings, common areas, division and map of units and description of intended usage. This is sometimes called declaration of covenants and restrictions.

Deed - Written instrument used to record or transfer property ownership. The deed transfers the property from the grantor to the grantee. The most common type of real estate deeds are the general warranty, special warranty, bargain & sale, quitclaim and grant deeds. A variety of special purpose deeds used in many states include administrator's, executor's, sheriff's, guardian's, referee's, tax, trustee's, trust, release and gift deeds, as well as the deed in trust and deed in lieu of foreclosure .

Deed of Conveyance - A legal instrument used to transfer a property's title.

Deed in Lieu of foreclosure - A real estate deed used to convey title to a property from the current owner to the owner's lender or creditor. This deed is normally used when the current owner is in default or foreclosure proceedings. By voluntarily surrendering the property, both parties avoid the costs and delay of further legal proceedings. The lender receives title without going through the usual court and auction process; in exchange, the loan is terminated. Similar to the power of sale clause, this is a type of non-judicial foreclosure .

Deed in Trust - A legal instrument used to establish a land trust and transfer property into it. The grantor conveys the property to the trustee. Note that the deed in trust is different from a deed of trust.

Deed of Reconveyance - See Trustee's Deed entry.

Deed of Release - See Release Deed entry.

Deed of Trust - A type of mortgage deed in which a third party holds the title in trust as a security, while the borrower continues to make payments to the lender. Most residential mortgage lenders will not allow the loan to close while the subject property is in a trust. The loan programs that will close with a trust normally use a deed of trust. The borrower conveys the legal title to the trustee, who retains the property until the debt to the lender is paid in full. If the borrower defaults, the trustee may sell the subject property to satisfy the debt, without benefit of foreclosure proceedings. Note that the deed of trust is different from the deed in trust.

Deed Restriction - A clause in the deed that restricts the use of the property. For example, a residential property normally cannot be converted into a commercial property. Deed restrictions placed by developers to control the quality or aesthetics of a subdivision are often called restrictive covenants. Note that when zoning and restrictions conflict, whichever is more restrictive is usually followed. Unlawful deed restrictions are unenforceable.

Default - Failure to meet or perform a contract obligation. With mortgage loans, the lender may declare the loan in default any time after a payment becomes past due beyond the grace period. However, most lenders will not declare default until the borrower is at least one to three months behind. A default notice will activate the foreclosure proscriptions of the mortgage deed.

Default Clause - The promissory notes of mortgage loans typically have default clauses that allow lenders to exercise its option to accelerate scheduled payments or foreclose the subject property.

Defeasance Clause - In title theory states, the defeasance clause is a mortgage provision or clause allowing the borrower to regain his or her property when the loan is fully paid.

Defect in Title - See Title Defect entry.

Deferred Interest - When the monthly payment is insufficient to satisfy the interest rate charge, the difference is added to the principal balance as negative amortization. This deferred interest increases (rather than decrease) the principal balance.

Deferred Interest Mortgage (DIM) - A mortgage loan that involves deferred interest, because the interest actually charged and collected is insufficient to satisfy the interest due on the loan. This typically resuts in negative amortization. Some GPM and ARM loans with payment caps may have deferred interest characteristics.

Deferred Maintenance - Property repair, maintenance and improvement requirements that have been delayed. Such maintenance are ones that are considered mandatory, but have not been performed. Deferred maintenance often occurs in properties that are under-performing or do not generate enough cash to meet all repair and maintenance needs.

Deficiency Judgment - A court order stating that the borrower's obligations continue to be in default and payable. For example, if a lender forecloses a property and sells it for a loss, that lender may apply for a deficiency judgment against the former borrower to recoup the loss. The deficiency judgment is a general judgment against the individual, rather than a specific judgment against a single property.

Degree of Operating Leverage - A rental property management calculation that displays the effect of new tenants on operating income. This measurement indicates the percentage change in net operating income that comes from a change in occupancy level.

Delinquency - Failure or inability to make loan payments according to the terms of the promissory note and mortgage deed. A delinquency can result in a finding and notice of default, which can eventually result in foreclosure.

Delivery and Acceptance - Legal real estate term referring to the actual time that a title to property is fully conveyed: when the grantor delivers and the grantee accepts the title. Silence by the grantee or the proper recording of the deed is legally considered acceptance. With escrow closings, the actual time of delivery and acceptance reverts to the time when the grantor delivers the title to the escrowee.

Demand Feature - The mortgage and promissory note clause that allows the lender to accelerate the loan and demand immediate, full repayment of the loan balance. The typical mortgage loan provides for a demand feature if the borrower defaults on the loan or the ownership of the property is ever altered or transferred.

Demised Property - Another term for leased properties. This legal term applies to premises or any portion of a real estate property whose interests or rights are temporarily transferred by the owner to another party. See the Lease entry.

Demising Clause - The formal provision in the lease through which the property owner (or its agent) leases the property to the tenant, and by which the tenant takes the property.

Demolition Clause - A provision in a lease indicating that when the ground lease expires, the building and its leased premises will be demolished.

Density - The average number of persons or units in a particular space. Zoning laws typically impose specific density limits, depending on the type of property. These density requirements, for example, will limit the number of houses in a typical block or the occupancy capacity of a proposed development.

Depreciable Basis - The amount in a property's value that may be depreciated. This is generally the basis less the value of the land.

Depreciable Life - This tax-related term refers to the number of years for which a property owner can depreciate the value of the property's improvements.

Depreciation - The loss or decrease in property value because of obsolescence, wear and tear, economic factors or age. Depreciation has functional, economic and tax elements. In appraisals, the three classes of depreciation used in the cost approach are physical deterioration, functional obsolescence and economic obsolescence. Such depreciation can be further labeled curable or incurable.

Under standard actual cash value coverage, insurance policies will deduct depreciation from original cost when calculating reimbursements. For tax deduction purposes, however, depreciation can only be taken on property used in a business, trade or income generation. Personal residences cannot claim depreciation deductions. Depreciation deductions can be calculated with either the straight line method or accelerated cost recovery system.

Derogatory Credit Entries - Sometimes referred to as "derogatories," these are any negative items—such as late payments, collections, judgments or inquiries—on a credit report.

Descent - Legal term for situation in which the property owner dies without the subject property being included in a will. The property is then acquired, usually by the government or a court-appointed administrator, through descent.

Design Development - The stage and process during a development project, during which the architect completes the plans and specifications for the proposed development. This stage usually begins after the architect's initial schematic design has been approved by the developer.

Designated Agent - In the real estate market, the salespeople who work for a broker and are authorized to act as agent for a seller or buyer--as designated by the broker.

Deteriorating Area - A real estate industry term referring to areas whose properties display marked neglect, disrepair and subsequent decrease in relative demand.

Determinable Fee - See the Fee Simple Defeasible entry.

Developer - An individual or entity who undertakes the transformation of undeveloped or underdeveloped land into an improved property.

Development - The improvement of a property. Development may entail everything from subdividing large plats, creating infrastructure improvements and constructing the buildings.

Development Contract - An agreement by which a developer agrees to construct a particular improvement and the client agrees to purchase the improvement and (normally) property upon completion.

Development Loan - Funds loaned for infrastructure improvements (building of streets or utilities, etc.) to make property suitable for sale or construction.

Devise - The act of conveying title to a property through a will.

Dimension Lumber - The standardized type of load-supporting lumber used for most construction as girders, joists, planks, posts, rafters and studs. Dimension lumber is typically 2" to 5" thick and up to 12" wide.

Diminishing Return - An investment term referring to the relationship between the cost of an investment or improvement and the value it adds, in which the value increases less than the amount of the investment.

Direct Participation Program - A real estate investment program, in which investors participate directly in the cash flow and tax benefits of an investment. Such a program, for example, would pass-through much of the property's operating profits and allowable tax deductions to the investors.

Disbursement - The release of funds. With a purchase mortgage, the closing agent disburses the loan proceeds at the conclusion of the closing. However, if a borrower is refinancing a primary residential property, the disbursement must be delayed three business days. This three-day delay is called the "Rescission Period," and allows the borrower to reconsider and possibly cancel the refinance loan.

Discharge Date - With bankruptcies, the discharge date is the official date on which the bankruptcy filing is formally ended. When a bankruptcy is discharged, the bankruptcy reorganization or disbursement is completed and bankruptcy protection ends.

Disclosure - A release of information. Real estate transactions normally require the seller to disclose specific information about the subject property. Mortgage loans require the lender to provide the borrower with several government- required disclosures.

Discount Fee, Points - The discount fee is a charge by the lender and can be assessed as either a dollar amount or as points (percentage of the loan amount). The discount fee is normally charged in conjunction with a lowering of the interest rate.

Discount Rate - The measurement of the difference between the current cost of money and future cost of money. It is used in the discounted cash flow analysis to determine the present value of future projected cash flow.

Discounted Cash Flow - A financial expression of the estimated current value of future cash flow. This measurement helps to estimate the current value of a property, based on its future earnings. By comparing this current value estimate with the projected development cost, the real estate investor can analyze the profitability of the investment. This calculation begins with the projected future cash flow, and then reduces that cash flow by the discount rate.

E

Earnest Money - Portion of the down payment delivered to the seller or an escrow agent as evidence of good faith so as to legally bind the purchase. When a purchase contract is offered and accepted by the seller, the buyer must typically provide an earnest money deposit. This deposit will be credited to the buyer's account, at the time of closing, as a portion of the down payment. [A typical earnest money requirement with many residential purchases is at least $1,000 at the time of signing and up to 5% of the entire purchase price within a few days after contract review.]

Easement - A right to use the land of another person for a specific purpose, such as for a right-of-way or utilities. For example, a utility company may obtain a right-of-way across a private property when deemed necessary by the local community. Easements can be positive or negative; they are also either appurtenant or in gross.

Easement by Necessity - An easement created by law or the court, especially to provide access to landlocked property owners.

Easement by Prescription - A method of establishing an involuntary easement allowed by most states. By openly and continuously using someone's land without consent for a number of years, a neighboring landowner may obtain an easement through his neighbor's property.

Easement In Gross - A type of easement right that is held by individuals and normally terminate with the death of one of the parties involved. For example, a farmer gets an easement (in gross) right to store some equipment on her neighbor's adjacent lot. If either the farmer or her neighbor dies, the easement right ends. The most common form is the commercial easement in gross.

Eave - The bottom portion of the roof's exposed overhang.

Economic Base - The underlying commercial and industrial components on an area that provides employment and revenue to the area.

Economic Conversion - The process of converting a property's usage—with subsequent renovations—to a different use. For example, an industrial loft warehouse may be converted into stylish apartments. If the profits justify the cost, this would be a good economic conversion.

Economic Depreciation - The decrease in a property's value caused by external forces. For example, a loss of the major employer in an area can affect the demand for new residential and retail developments in that area.

Economic Feasibility Study - An analysis of a proposed investment that focuses on the economic and financial factors that will affect the subject property and influence the investment's future success.

Economic Life - The projected length of time that a property, building or improvement can be expected to satisfy the demands of its intended use or application.

Economic Obsolescence - Also called external obsolescence, the type of obsolescence that occurs when a property or element of a property loses its value or attractiveness to the market. All economic obsolescence are always incurable.

Effective Age - In contrast to a building or improvement's chronological age, the effective age considers the property's age based on wear and tear. For example, a poorly maintained building may only be 30 years, but the unchecked deterioration could give it an effective age of 60 years. This neglected building would thus physically resemble a maintained building twice its age.

Effective Gross Income - This projected amount is the scheduled gross income and other miscellaneous revenues, less the projected vacancy rate.

Effective Monthly Income - For income qualifying purposes, this is the gross monthly income amount used to qualify the applicant. Effective monthly income must come from a stable and acceptable source, such as regular employment, investments or court-ordered judgments. Undocumented income is normally not acceptable.

Efflorescence - White deposit sometimes found on brick walls.

Egress - Access from a property to an exit or public road.

Electrified Floor - A method of interior design that runs power and telephone lines beneath the floor of each building level. This design allows quick installation of phone and electric outlets at more points with fewer visible wiring.

Emblements - Cultivated annual crops, which are considered personal property. See Fruits of Industry entry.

Eminent Domain - A legal term referring to the power of the government to take land from private owners for public use. This is one of the four basic government powers of taxation, eminent domain, escheat and police powers. Congress later expanded this power of eminent domain to public utilities. When a property is taken from its private owner, the property is then legally condemned and the owner must be paid fair market rates or fair compensation. The government exercise its eminent domain power through condemnation.

Enabling Declaration -see the Declaration of Condominium entry.

Enabling Legislation - Specific legislation by state governments that gives local governments (county or municipality) the authority to exercise certain government powers, such as taxation or police powers. However, some local governments receive those powers through Home Rule Powers in the state's constitution.

Encroachment - Any structure or object that protrudes beyond a property's legal boundary, into a neighboring property. The encroachment must be corrected or be insured by the title insurance before a mortgage loan can be closed for its purchase or financing. For example, if your fence is accidentally built on your neighbor's property then that fence is an encroachment. Even if your neighbor allows it, the title company must insure this encroachment or obtain a "hold harmless" letter before concluding the settlement.

Encumbrance - Any legal claim, charge, liability, intrusion, restriction or obstruction against property ownership. Encumbrances affect the marketability of the property and, thus, its value. For example, past due tax and mortgage liens are considered encumbrances because property ownership cannot be fully sold and transferred unless those items are completely paid or somehow addressed. Other types of encumbrances include zoning ordinances, easement rights, restrictive covenants and claims.

End Loan - Sometimes called a permanent loan, the end loan refers to a long-term refinance loan that pays off a short-term construction loan.

Energy Efficient Glass - See Low Emissivity Glass entry.

English Tudor - See Tudor entry.

Entertainment Property - Real estate indstry term referring to a type of retail property used for entertainment purposes. This can run the gamut from movie theaters to amusement parks. Note that this is not the same as recreeational property.

Entitlement - In the mortgage industry, this refers to a military veteran's available benefits with a VA-guaranteed loan.

Environmental Impact Statement - A report required by the EPA on all development projects to determine the impact of developments on the surrounding environment.

Environmental Protection Agency (EPA) - The EPA was established as an independent agency in 1970, charged with administering and enforcing environmental laws, including the Clean Air Act, National Environmental Policy Act, Clean Water Act, Resources Conservation & Recovery Act, Comprehensive Environmental Response, Compensation & Liability Act, Superfund Amendment & Reauthorization Act, Coastal Zone Management

Act and the Lead-Based Paint Hazard & Reduction Act.

EPA Endorsement - The guarantee issued by the title search company or attorney that the subject property is clear, according to the title search, of any potential environmental (pollution) violations, based on past zoning, usage or ownership.

Equal Credit Opportunity Act (ECOA) - A federal law that prohibits creditors, lenders and brokers from discriminating against an applicant on the basis of race, color, religion, national or ethnic origin, sex, age, marital status, receipt of income from public assistance programs, or past complaints based on the Consumer Credit Protection Act.

Equalizer - A formula or constant applied to real estate assessments, to assure state-wide or local equality when determining tax assessments.

Equitable Lien - Any lien established by the courts to ensure fairness or justice.

Equitable Title - The limited interest provided by a purchase agreement to a buyer who has agreed to purchase a property but has not closed on the transaction.

Equitable Right of Redemption - A property owner's interest in a real property that has been removed due to a mortgage default and/or foreclosure ; and the property owner's right to redeem the property from foreclosure .

Equity - The economic resource of the subject property owed to the property owner. More precisely, it is the portion of the property's value beyond the liabilities or liens against the property. Thus, a $120,000 home with $75,000 in mortgage liens has a net equity of approximately $45,000 ($120,000 - $75,000). If the property is ever sold, that is gross profit that the owner can anticipate.

Equity Build-Up - A property's net worth that is produced by the appreciation of the property's value and the simultaneous paying down of any mortgage debt.

Equity Dividend Rate - A rate of return measurement that analyzes the strength of a property's income stream. The equity dividend rate is derived from the before-tax cash flow divided by the property's equity.

Equity Kicker - A financing arrangement that provides the lender with a portion of the cash flow and/or resale proceeds. This is obviously a concession to persuade the lender to make the loan.

Equity Loan - A type of mortgage loan that converts a property's equity into cash. If this equity financing involves absorption or repayment of an existing mortgage lien—in addition to cashing equity—then it is often called a cash-out refinance loan.

Equity REIT - A type of real estate investment trust that invests in the ownership and management of real estate properties.

Erosion - The wearing away of land through either natural or artificial causes. This can have legal implications for real estate owners whose property abuts a body of water. Many real estate title will define the parcel's boundaries as ending at the water's edge. As land is eroded and the water's edge creeps further into the parcel, the actual parcel size begins to shrink.

Errors and Omissions Insurance - Insurance coverage obtained by brokers and agents to protect themselves from liabilities arising from errors, negligence and mistakes.

Escalation, Escalator Clause - The right of a lender to increase the interest rate of an adjustable rate loan agreement. For example, ARM loans have escalation rights that allow the lender to adjust the loan's interest rate once every period or based on the movement of an index.

Escheat - A legal doctrine by which property reverts to the state when there is no legal owner. This can occur whenever the property owner dies without an heir or legal claimant. If the owner dies without a will, a relative or other claimant can avoid the escheat by filing a claim for the property--and paying all the required taxes.

Escrow Account - Property or money held by a third party, usually a bank. Both the title company and the mortgage lender maintain different escrow accounts—sometimes called "impound" accounts. The title company's escrow account collects all closing funds and disburses them to satisfy liens and appropriate parties. With many purchases, the title company will often hold an impound account containing tax payments from and by the seller—which will be applied as soon as the next real estate tax bill arrives.

For residential mortgage purposes, the escrow is established and maintained by the lender to pay for future property taxes and insurance premiums. When it comes time to pay the property taxes and insurance premium, the lender will use the funds in the escrow.

Escrow Agent - A neutral individual who coordinates an escrow closing. The agent is usually someone from the title company, lender's escrow department or one of the representing attorneys.

Escrow Clause - The clause in insurance policies indicating the lender (mortgagee) and its assignees as beneficiaries of the insurance policy. If the subject property is destroyed, the insurer will normally first pay off the existing mortgage balance before disbursing any surplus insurance claims to the home owner. The exception would be if the insurance disbursements were earmarked directly toward reconstruction. Otherwise, lenders may be left holding the bag for a large mortgage balance on a property now worth only the land.

Escrow Closing - A commonly used method of closing in which not all of the parties are present. The parties involved enter into an escrow agreement, and the escrow agent will typically obtain assurances of marketable title, collect all require funds and documents, deposit and disburse funds and record all pertinent deeds and documents. With escrow closings, the official date of title conveyance is when the title was delivered to the escrow.

Escrow Disclosure - Informational notice detailing the current and projected escrow collections and disbursements. This disclosure is normally provided to the borrower during the loan closing.

Escrow Waiver - With the payment of an escrow waiver fee, qualified borrowers may forego the escrow requirements. With many conforming loans, the borrower may waive the escrow requirement if the loan is only at 75% LTV ratio or below—at least 25% down payment or equity. The lender may still re-impose the escrow requirement at a later time if the borrower proves subsequently delinquent in paying property taxes and insurance premiums.

Escrowee - The managing agent of an escrow. With escrow closings, the escrowee receives and holds the different assets, properties and consideration until ready for proper distribution or delivery.

Escutcheon - The decorative plate around door knobs, locks and pipes passing through a wall or floor.

Estate - In the real estate industry, the term estate refers to the interest an individual has in real property. The term estate encompasses the degree, nature and extent of ownership rights. Estates are generally divided into two groups: freehold estates of indefinite length and leasehold estates for a fixed term.

Estate at Sufferance - Commonly called Tenancy at Sufferance, this legal term applies to the unpermitted occupancy by a tenant of a property after the lease term has expired.

Estate at Will - Legal term describing the permitted occupancy of a property--with or without a lease agreement--for an unspecified term. This arrangement can be terminated by either the owner or tenant at any time.

Estate for Life - Legal term referring to an interest in a property that terminates upon the death of a specified individual.

Estate for Years - Legal term referring to an interest in a property for a specified period of time. This is the most common type of leasehold estate. The lessee must vacate at end of the lease term or otherwise becomes a holdover tenant. Sale of property or death normally does not end a lease.

Estate from Period to Period - See Periodic Estate entry.

Estate in Reversion - An estate left by a grantor that begins after the termination of estate granted by that individual.

Estate Tax - The tax assessment based on the value of a property left by a decedent.

Estoppel Letter - A legal letter confirming the current facts of an agreement or transaction. At most closings, the borrower will sign an estoppel letter confirming the transaction and loan amounts. The estoppel is a legal concept that prohibits a party from denying facts that were once acknowledged by a person as true and accepted by others as factual.

Evaporator - A device found in many cooling systems that receives water from a condenser. The evaporator converts the cooled water from the condenser into cold water vapor. Air or water is then passed over coils in the evaporator before being forced to rooms that need to be cooled.

Eviction - The process of terminating the occupancy of a tenant. Actual evictions are initiated by the landlord; while constructive evictions are initiated by the tenant.

Eviction Notice - A formal notice provided by a landlord to a tenant who is currently in default on either the lease terms or rental obligations.

Evidence of Title - Documented proof of valid ownership interest and right to convey title. Evidence is not a guarantee, but they offer proof acceptable in most transactions. The four most common types of evidence of title are abstract of title with attorney's opinion, Torrens certificate, certificate of title and title insurance.

Excavation - Usually, the first step in building on land. This prepares the ground by removing earth and ensuring that it is sufficiently flat and firm.

Exchange - A tax-free exchange of similar properties, permitted under Section 1031 of the Internal Revenue Code.

Exclusive Listing - A type of listing agreement between sellers and real estate agents that gives the listing agent exclusivity among all other real estate agents. However, the seller can avoid paying any commissions if the seller finds the buyer without assistance from the seller. If the property is sold through any other real estate agent, the listing agent receives a commission from the seller. Compare this to open listing (non-exclusive) and exclusive right of sale (totally exclusive).

Exclusive Right of Sale, Exclusive Right to Sell - A type of listing agreement between sellers and real estate agents that commits the buyer to pay commission to the listing agent when the property is sold, regardless if the property is sold through the listing or without any agents. Compare this to open listing (non-exclusive) and exclusive listing (somewhat exclusive).

Exculpatory Clause - A provision in a mortgage or lease agreement holding harmless the lender or landlord for losses suffered by the borrower or tenant in relation to the subject property or agreement. Most states prohibit or limit such clauses in leases.

F

Façade - The exterior front of a building.

Face Value - The dollar amount indicated on a contract, security or or financial instrument. The face value often differs from the cash value of an instrument. For example, a life insurance policy may have a face value of $100,000 but have a current cash value equal to a portion of the insured person's deposit to date.

Factory Outlet - A retail store owned and operated by a manufacturer for the purpose of marketing the manufacturer's products directly to the public.

Fair Compensation - When the government exercises its eminent domain powers and takes property through condemnation procedures, the property owner must receive fair market value and necessary compensation.

Fair Credit Reporting Act - A 1977 federal legislation that regulates credit reporting agencies and the access to and use of consumer credit data. Credit bureaus can only provide access by court order or, with the consumer's permission, for credit, insurance and employment. Also, credit bureaus must correct or remove errors brought to their attention and provide file data to the consumer. Lenders who reject an application because of adverse credit information, must inform the borrower about the source of that information and make credit information on file available.

Fair Housing Act of 1968 - Actually contained in Title 8 of the Civil Rights Act of 1968, this federal legislation expanded the fair housing coverage reestablished with CRA 1964. It was subsequently amended in 1988 to ban discrimination on the basis of race, skin color, national origin, gender, familial status and physical or mental handicap. This act also prohibited discriminatory advertising practices.

Fair Market Value - Real estate term referring to the price or estimated value that most accurately reflect market supply and demand conditions.

Fannie Mae (FNMA) - See the Federal National Mortgage Association entry.

Farmers Home Administration (FmHA) - A government agency within the U.S. Department of Agriculture, that administers assistance to buyers of homes and farms in rural areas.

Fascia - The outer beams of a rafter or the outer end joist attached to the ends of rafter beams. The outermost rafter beams that are the most exposed to the exterior is normally called fascia rafters.

Fashion-Oriented Center - A retail shopping mall containing primarily apparel, boutique, handcraft and often high-end specialty stores.

Feasibility Study - An investigation to examine anticipated results of a development or improvement project, with the goal of determining the potential and probability of success. Developers should always conduct at least a preliminary feasibility study before investing large sums into a potentially money-losing effort.

Federal Deposit Insurance Corporation (FDIC) - A public corporation established by the U.S. government in 1933 for the purpose of regaining and maintaining consumer confidence in commercial banks. The FDIC insures individual deposits in commercial banks up to $100,000 for each depositor.

Federal Emergency Management Agency (FEMA) - This federal agency is most widely known for its task of responding to disaster assessment and relief. However, they also perform a crucial, preemptory task for the real estate market by determining flood zones and drawing the flood map. Properties that are located in a FEMA-determined flood zone will not receive residential mortgage financing, unless the borrower purchase federally subsidized, but still expensive flood insurance.

Federal Home Loan Mortgage Corporation (FHLMC) - Better known as "Freddie Mac," the FHLMC is a quasi-government agency and publicly traded company that raises money to purchase mortgage loans from lenders through the sale of FHLMC-guaranteed mortgage participation certificates (PCs). Similar to Fannie Mae (FNMA), Freddie Mac plays an important connection for the flow of funds between the financial investment market (supply) and loan borrowers (demand). Because of Fannie Mae and Freddie Mac, more funds are made available for the housing market—thus making homeownership generally more affordable.

Federal Housing Administration (FHA) - An office of the Department of Housing and Urban Development. Through the FHA loan , the FHA encourages lending to low-income Americans by ensuring certain loans made by qualified lenders. The FHA does not fund loans, it merely acts as an alternative type of mortgage insurance to protect FHA lenders from losses on FHA loans.

Federal National Mortgage Association (FNMA) - "Fannie Mae" is a publicly listed corporation that supports the secondary mortgage market by purchasing conventional mortgages, as well as FHA- and VA-backed loans, from lenders nationwide. FNMA then packages and resells these loans as securities. Similar to Freddie Mac (FHLMC), Fannie Mae plays an important connection for the flow of funds between the financial investment market (supply) and loan borrowers (demand). Because of Fannie Mae and Freddie Mac, more funds are made available for the housing market—thus making homeownership generally more affordable.

Federal Reserve Bank, System - The Fed was established in 1913 by the U.S. Congress to manage the nation's credit infrastructure and fiscal stability. It does so by controlling its discount rate, reserve requirements and open market activities. The country is divided into 12 districts, with a district reserve bank, whose governors are the core directors of the federal reserve board.

Fee Simple - Fee simple is an Old English word for the type of property ownership that provides permanent and absolute ownership of property— as compared to a lease. Landholders transferred property by granting an estate, then called a "fee," to a vassal or other person for money or services.

Fee Simple Absolute - A real estate term referring to the highest form of ownership--complete and indefinite ownership, subject only to government regulation. This is one of the two types of inheritable freehold estates; compare with fee simple defeasible.

Fee Simple Defeasible - A real estate term referring to one of the two types of inheritable or fee simple freehold estates. Sometimes called determinable fee, conditional fee or qualified fee, fee simple defeasible estates are subject to conditions of when the estate will begin or end. Depending on whether the fee simple defeasible is subject to condition precedent or subject to condition subsequent, this estate terminates when approved conditions end or when prohibited uses arise. When a fee simple defeasible ends, the title passes by one of three possibilities: a reversion interest to the original grantor; a reversion interest to the grantor's heir; or a remainder interest to a specified third part.

Felt Paper - Sheet paper commonly used in construction for roofing and sheathing against moisture or dampness.

Fenestration - The design and placement of windows in a building. [Trivia note: defenestration means to throw someone or something through a window.]

Feudal System - The precursor to modern allodial system of ownership, feudal system placed ownership of all lands in royal hands, with some exceptions for clerical or religious properties.

FHA Loan - A loan insured by the Federal Housing Administration (FHA). FHA does not provide loan funds, it insures qualified loans by accepted residential lenders—making FHA a form of mortgage insurance.

G-I

Gable - The triangular section atop the side exterior walls, between the sloping roofs.

Gable Roof - The most common type of roofing used in most residential homes today. The basic gable roof consists of two sloping roofs attached to a central ridge board running through the center- top of the roof frame. Unlike a hipped roof, the gable roof has vertical gables at the ends of the roof skeletons.

Gain - An increase in the value of property or assets. See Capital Gain entry.

Galvanized - Iron or steel elements that has been coated with zinc

Gambrel Roof - A variation of the gable roof seen in many old- fashion barns. The gambrel's roof still use a central ridge board and gables on the ends. However, the gambrel actually has four slopes instead of the gable's normal two. Each side of the roof actually contains two slopes dropping from the ridge board, with the lower one having a very steep incline.

Gap Loan - Additional mortgage financing that fills a shortfall or spread with the current mortgage loan.

Garden Apartment - Real estate term for an apartment unit on the ground floor or basement level.

Gas Lease - Similar to oil leases, a landowner may give another party the right to drill for gas on that landowner's property. If no gas is found, the landowner receives a flat rent. If the lessee discovers gas and begins extraction, the landowner receives royalty payments, often in addition to the flat rent. Sometimes, gas and oil lease rights are combined.

General Agent - A type of agency relationship, often created by a general power of attorney, that allows the agent to bind the principal to contracts within the specified scope of the agency. For example, a property manager act on behalf of the principal, within the specific scope of managing the principal's property.

General Contractor - The contractor primarily responsible for supervising a construction or improvement project. The property owner or developer works with the GC, who will then hire, manage and pay subcontractors (as well as the GC's own employees) to complete the project.

General Lien - A lien against both personal and real property of a borrower. Compare to specific lien.

General Listing - See Open Listing entry.

General Partner - The partner or partners in a general or limited partnership who possess the right to participate in the management of the partnership.

General Partnership - A form of partnership in which the general partners possess the right to participate in the management of the partnership. However, general partners have the disadvantage of unlimited liability for all of the partnership's debts.

General Power of Attorney - A type of power of attorney relationship in which the attorney or agent is charged with and authorized to enter into contracts and agreements on behalf of the principal within the defined scope of the agency.

General Warranty Deed - A deed that provides the buyer (grantee) with the greatest level of protection against potential problems with the property's title through specific seller guarantees in covenants, which include seisin, against encumbrances , quiet enjoyment, further assurance and warranty forever

Geodetic Survey System – See the Rectangular Survey System entry.

Georgian - Traditional style of housing that emphasized symmetry. The front door and chimneys are normally centered and windows are evenly spaced. When wings are attached, they are typically identical. This traditional style has been adapted to many contemporary styles.

German Lap Siding - See Drop Siding entry.

Ghetto - An area of a city populated predominantly by a minority group, who are forced to occupy that area because of social, legal, economic or racial pressure from the majority.

Gift Deed - A type of deed used to convey title to property as part of a gift.

Gift Letter, Affidavit - A document from the gift-giver, which states that there is no expressed or implied obligation to repay the gift. If the buyer is obtaining a gift for all or a portion of the down payment, closing costs or reserve requirements, then the donor must sign a gift letter confirming the gift status of the provided funds. In addition, the donor must often provide documentation that the funds actually belong to the donor and is transferred from the donor's account into the applicant's possession.

Ginnie Mae - Popular name for the Government National Mortgage Association.

Girder - Horizontal beams used to support joists or flooring. Wooden girders are normally at least 4x4 beams. Metal girders are often I-beams.

Glazing - The process of placing glass in a window or frame.

Good Faith Estimate (GFE) - The good faith estimate must be provided to the applicant within three days of the application. The GFE itemizes the costs and expenses that the borrower will incur with the processing and closing of the loan.

Government Lot - With the rectangular survey system, areas smaller than full quarter sections are designated as government lots and are numbered and placed in the fractional sections along the northern and western boundaries of the township.

Government National Mortgage Association (GNMA) - Also known as "Ginnie Mae," this government agency functions in the secondary market but does not purchase mortgage loans; instead it approves "loan poolers" and issues government guarantees for certain FHA, VA or Farmers Home Administration (FmHA) loans. Ginnie Mae is similar to Freddie Mac and Fannie Mae, except that Ginnie Mae concentrates on government, non-conventional loans.

Government Survey System - See the Rectangular Survey System entry.

Grace Period - The time between the due date and the past- due date of a loan during which there is no late charge. If a payment is still not received after the grace period (usually 10-15 days), the lender will assess a late charge on the overdue amount. The borrower is technically in default after the grace period expires.

Graduated Lease Payment - A type of variable lease arrangement whose payments increase over the term at predetermined rates. Compare with the index lease.

Graduated Payment Adjustable Rate Mortgage (GPARM, GPAM) - A mortgage repayment plan that provides for lower initial monthly payments, which increase annually until the mortgage becomes a fully amortized ARM loan. This is a variation of the GPM loan.

Graduated Payment Mortgage (GPM) - This payment plan offers lower monthly payments during the first year(s), after which the payments increase annually until reaching a level that fully amortizes the loan within its term.

Grandfather Clause - An exemption to a new ordinance or law for a specific property or person. For example, new laws may require specific zoning and building code restrictions for a neighborhood. Existing properties in that neighborhood will not have to make the changes required to meet new codes; however, those same properties may face additional restrictions if they try to make any later improvements.

Grant Deed - A type of deed similar to special warranty deeds, in which the grantor limits the covenant against encumbrances to claims incurred only while the grantor owned the property.

Grantee - With the typical deed, the buyer or recipient of any conveyance of property is normally called the grantee. Legal capacity and the grantee's signature are not required; however, the grantee must be alive when the deed is delivered.

Granting Clause - Also called words of conveyance, this clause is part of most deeds. It identifies the type of deed and type of ownership being conveyed, as well as states the grantor's intent to convey title to the grantee.

Grantor - With the typical deed, the seller, current owner or provider of any conveyance is normally considered the grantor. Most states require that deed grantors be legally competent and be clearly and accurately identified in the deed.

Gravel Stop - The metal strip around the roof's edge.

Gravity Circulation System (Heat) - A type of heating system that uses gravity to distribute heat to the different parts of a building. There are actually four common types of gravity systems, all of which require a separate air-conditioning system: gravity warm air, pipeless warm air, gravity hot water and steam heating.

Gravity Hot Water System - A type gravity heating system that uses hot water to heat areas and rooms in a building. The boiler pipes heated water to radiators and then pipes the cooled water back to the boiler for reheating. Radiators distribute heat through convection. Hot-water heating systems are simple to operate, but respond slowly to sudden rises or drops in outdoor temperatures.

Gravity Warm Air System - An efficient type of gravity heating system that is ideal for cottages and smaller homes. The furnace is centrally placed below and between the rooms to be heated, to minimize duct lengths. Exploiting the principle that warm air rises and cold air sinks, warm-air registers are placed on the wall and cold-air return grills are placed on the floor. The system will also require a small fresh-air intake from outdoors and a humidifier. Unfortunately, this system requires much space for ducts and often distributes heat unevenly.

Green Card - Common name for the permanent resident alien registration card, issued by the Immigration & Naturalization Service, to immigrants who are given full resident status in the U.S. Immigrants with green cards are eventually allowed to apply for naturalization, to become U.S. citizens..

Green Lumber - Construction term referring to lumber and wood construction material with moisture content over 19%. Lumber used in residential and other construction is graded according to moisture content and structural quality as established by the National Grade Rule. Compare with Dry Lumber entry.

Gross Floor Area - The measurement of the total floor area in a building, including core, common and vacant spaces.

Gross Income - The total income for a given period of time, before taxes and other deductions. When qualifying an applicant for a residential loan, the pre-tax and pre-deduction gross income

amount is used to determine the Debt-to- Income ratio.

Gross Income Allowance - When residential rental income-producing properties are involved, the gross income allowance is the calculation of gross income for qualification purposes. Most residential loans allow 75% of the rental income from the subject property's apartment unit to be added to the applicant's gross income. For example, if you are earning $3,000 per month and you wish to buy a two-flat with rental income from one rental unit (assuming you will live in the other unit) of $800 per month, you will use a gross monthly income of $3,600 ($3,000 plus 75% of gross rental) for debt-to-income qualification purposes.

Gross Income Multiplier - A calculation rate used with the income approach to estimating value, particularly for commercial, industrial and larger residential apartment properties. It is used instead of the gross rent multiplier because such larger facilities often generate revenue from other non- rent incomes.

Gross Lease - A lease agreement in which the tenant pays one constant payment, with no additions for the landlord's operating expenses. However, gross leases--which are the most common type for residential properties--does not include tenant utilities, unless specifically stated in the lease.

Gross Leasable Area - The sum measurement of all area available for tenant rental. It is usually measured from the center of border partitions and consists of all space on which rental income can be collected. In contrast to the usable area, gross leasable area includes common areas, hallways, exterior walls and entrances.

Gross Potential Income - The sum total of all projected rental income, assuming no vacancy.

Gross Profit Ratio - A ratio that displays a rate of return measurement for installment purchases. This calculation is the gross profit from an installment sale divided by the contract price.

Gross Rent Multiplier (GRM) - The GRM is a factoring tool used by the property appraiser to assess the market value of a property, under the income valuation approach. The multiplier is a rate based on the sales price divided by the gross monthly rent of comparable properties. This multiplier is then applied to the market rent of the subject property to estimate the value of that property. For example, if an appraiser is analyzing a four-flat and discovers that similar four-flats in the area have market values that are 10.5 times their market rents, the appraiser will use a GRM of 105. Applied to the subject property, the appraiser will multiply the subject property's market rental income by 10.5 to estimate the property's value via the income approach. Commercial, industrial and larger residential properties use the gross income multiplier system.

Gross Rental Income - The total rental revenue generated, prior to any taxes, operating expenses or deductions.

Gross Revenue - The total of all income being generated by an income-producing property.

Ground Lease - A lease arrangement for raw land. Most are long-term (40-90 years) net leases, allowing for the lessee to recoup the investment costs of improving the land and building upon it.

Grout - Plaster-like material used to seal joints, especially with tiles that need to be water- resistant.

Growing Equity Mortgage (GEM) - A loan in which the normal payment is increased each year so that the amortization is accelerated, thus paying off the mortgage in a shorter period of time.

Guardian's Deed - A type of deed used by a legally appointed guardian to convey title to property owned by the guardian's ward.

Guide Meridian - Going north-to-south, guide meridians are used with the rectangular survey system to compensate for the curvature of the earth. Every fourth principal meridian is a guide meridian that is shorter than the standard principal meridian.

Gusset Plate - Construction term referring to metal or wood plates used to connect the rafters, studs and beams in a truss roof. Gusset plates offer additional support, instead of simply nailing two beams together. For example, gusset plates are used in truss roofs at the corners where rafters connect to each other or where rafters connect to the lower chord.

Gutter - Construction term referring to the artificial channel attached to bottom ends of sloping roofs. Gutters prevent uncontrolled waterfalls and potential damage to the building by directing rainwater to downspouts. The term gutter can also refer to the channel along the edge of streets that direct water to storm drains.

Gypsum Board - A plasterboard with paper covering. See Drywall entry.

Habendum Clause - An element of a deed that defines or limits the estate being conveyed by the grantor to the grantee. This must correspond with the granting clause; if not, the granting clause takes precedence.

Hacienda - See Spanish Colonial entry.

Handyman Special - Real estate industry euphemism for properties that need significant rehab or improvement. They are usually priced lower to factor in the needed work. The term is often a nice way of saying the property is currently a dump but can be repaired to a habitable condition with increased value.

Hard Assets - A classification of assets referring to non-liquid assets, primarily real and personal properties. See liquid assets for more information.

Hard Construction Cost - The cost of constructing a building shell with most of the covering material. This amount excludes much of the mechanical equipment and interior finishes.

Hazard Insurance - More commonly known as the homeowners insurance, the hazard insurance on the subject property covers physical damage due to accidents and acceptable hazards. Note that many hazard insurance policies require separate coverage for events such as flood, earthquake or hurricane.

Header - The wide horizontal framing planks or beams used to frame a window, door or wall. They are used to support the free ends of floor joists, studs or rafters, by transferring the roof and floor weight to the studs.

Hearth - The area around a fireplace, which basically extends the fireplace masonry floor. The hearth protects the floor area around the fireplace from sparks and ashes.

Heat Pump - A developing method of heating and cooling, which is proving highly efficient. During the winter, heat pumps can pump air or liquid through underground pipes; since the ground below the frost line retains a steady temperature, the air or water is heated (relative to outside air) by the ground. During the summer, the ground acts to cool the air and liquid running through the tubes.

Hectare - An area measurement equal to 107,637 square feet or 2.471 acres.

Heir - In the real estate industry, the heir is the individual who inherits interests or rights to a property.

High-Rise - The general definition of a high-rise structure is any building that contains seven or more stories. Buildings with four to six stories are normally considered mid-rise structures.

Highest and Best Use - A real estate term that projects the best economic use with respect to what is legally and physically possible for the property.

Hipped Roof - A roof design that replaces the gables with roofing slopes at the ends. The hipped roof has the two basic slopes dropping aside from the central ridge board. However, instead of gables, the hipped roof also has roof slopes at the ends the roof--giving it four roof slopes with no gables.

Historic Structure - Any building or improvement that is officially recognized by a government agency or government-chartered body as having historic significance. Properties that are officially designated historic usually face special improvement restrictions but also often receive tax incentives.

Hold Harmless - The act of indemnifying a person or entity from liabilities that my be incurred from a specific issue.

Hold Harmless Letter - Also called an indemnification affidavit, the hold harmless letter is a legal document in which one party assumes from another party all liability for a subject issue. The person or entity issuing the hold harmless letter assumes all obligations for liabilities that may arise from the specific issue. The person or entity receiving the hold harmless guarantee is theoretically freed from all obligations for liabilities arising from the specific issue.

In the context of title company closings, a hold harmless letter is required when the current title report indicates title blemishes—such as a lien that should already have been released— that were supposedly handled by the previous title company's closing. The previous title company would then issue a hold harmless letter exempting the current title company from risk with regard to the specific issue.

Hold-Back - Funds retained until certain events occur. For example, a lessee may negotiate a rent hold-back to ensure landlord's completion of agreed fit-up. Once the improvements are completed, the tenant will release the funds to the landlord.

Holder in Due Course - An individual or entity who acquires a bearer instrument and is eligible to keep it even though it may have been stolen.

Holding Area - The temporary storage area of a property's loading and receiving docks, where deliveries to tenants are parked.

Holding Costs - See Carrying Costs entry.

Holdover Provision - See Broker Protection Clause entry.

Holdover Tenant, Holdover Tenancy - Real estate term for lessee or lease condition that retains interest in a property even after the lease agreement has terminated.

Holographic Will - A will that is created by the testator in writing, but not witnessed. Many, but not all, states recognize holographic wills as valid.

Home Equity Line of Credit (HELOC) - A mortgage loan similar to the home equity loan but provides a credit line instead of a lump-sum loan. The borrower receives a check book—instead of a single check—and can make several disbursements against the credit line. The HELOC is assessed interest charges based on the current loan amount. The HELOC acts similar to credit cards, but its interest can be tax-deductible because it is considered a home mortgage loan.

Home Equity Loan - A junior mortgage refinance loan that is taken out against the equity that a homeowner has accrued on his or her property. For example, if a person owns a $200,000 home with a mortgage of $110,000 (for an established equity level of $90,000), that person can usually obtain a home equity loan for up to $90,000 or more. The home equity loan will not touch or affect the existing first mortgage, and this home equity loan will have a separate payment program.

Home Warranty - A type of property insurance coverage that cover repairs or replacements for the electric and mechanical systems of a home. Sellers and developers may take out such coverage to entice buyers.

Homeowners Association (HOA) - The collection of homeowners—and, when applicable, the project management team—of a condominium, townhouse or planned unit development (PUD) community. The HOA is responsible for managing the common areas and the community as a whole, and normally consists of all individual unit owners.

Homeowners Association Budget - Projected itemization of operating income and expenditures for the homeowners association. This is a legal requirement for all homeowners associations.

Homeowners Association Dues - The assessments charged by the homeowner association.

Homeowners Association Declarations & By-laws - The rules and regulations promulgated by the homeowner association that will govern its structure. This is a legal requirement for all homeowners associations.

Homestead Life Estates - A form of legal life estate practiced in certain states that protects a portion of value of the homeowner's principal residence from certain debt judgments. Real estate taxes and mortgage obligations are typically exempted from the homestead exemption, and most mortgage loans and contracts will require the homeowners to waive their homestead rights.

Homestead Exemption - There are two definitions for this real estate term. First, many states offer differing homestead exemptions, which reserve and protect a portion of people's homes from bankruptcies and major judgments. A second definition of homestead exemption is a reduction in property tax assessments that many taxing authority offers to homeowners.

Homestead Life Estate - A type of legal life estate recognized in some states that protects a portion of value of the homeowner's principal residence from certain judgments for debt. States vary, but most exempt real estate taxes and mortgages from such protection.

Homestead, Waiver of - When a married person is financing a mortgage on his or her home as the sole borrower—which often happens when the other person's credit does not qualify—many lenders will require the non-borrowing spouse to sign a waiver of homestead to avoid future ownership issues, especially in case of default.

Hopper Window - A type of window in which the sash is hinged at the bottom while the top swings into the room. Unfortunately, this often interferes with drapes and blinds. It is best suited for basements. For more information about the parts and styles of windows, see the Windows entry.

Horizontal Property Laws - See Condominium Acts entry.

Horizontal Sliding Window - A type of window whose sashes slide horizontally, as opposed to the vertical double-hung windows. For more information about the parts and styles of windows, see the Windows entry.

Hot Water Tank & Heater - A system that heats and maintains a reserve of hot water for a building or area.

House Wrap - A building paper or flexible material placed over the external sheathing to provide additional protection and insulation. The exterior panels or sidings are then nailed or screwed through the wrap.

Housing and Urban Development (HUD) - The federal cabinet-level department responsible for housing and urban concerns. For mortgage purposes, HUD regulates the housing industry and operates the FHA.

Housing Codes - Regulations established by local governments intended to ensure minimum safety and sanitation standards.

Housing Debt Ratio - The monthly housing debt divided by the monthly gross income. This ratio is often used by lenders to qualify loan applicants.

Housing Expenses - The housing-related charges that the home owner must anticipate and pay. Total housing expenses normally include the principal and interest payments on the mortgage loan, plus any homeowner's insurance, mortgage insurance and property tax charges.

Housing Starts - A measure of building permits issued for new housing construction. Economists and investors review the periodic publication of housing starts to forecast the pace of real estate development for the coming months.

HUD-1 - The HUD-1 Settlement Statement is used for all residential transactions to provide a uniform method for recording the specific settlement entries. It was developed by the Department of Housing and Urban Development (HUD).

Humidifier - A device to increase the moisture (water) content of the air in a space or building. Humidity affects heating efficiency, because a little water can better conduct heat. For example, you can be cold in a temperature with 75- degree Fahrenheit and 10% humidity, but feel warm in a 68-degree temperature with 40% humidity.

HVAC - Acronym for "heating, ventilation & air conditioning" used in the building industry.

Hybrid REIT - A real estate investment trust that invests in both areas allowed by law: real estate mortgages and ownership of income-producing properties.

Impact Fee - A fee that many municipalities and counties assess on builders and developers who are adding improvements to an area. The impact fee is meant to address the added cost of expanded services and infrastructure improvements that any new construction may require.

Implied Agency - A type of agency relationship created by the action, conduct or statements of the principal and agent.

Implied Contract - A legally recognized contract established by actions taken, even if the contract is not written or spoken.

Implied Warranty - A legally recognized warranty established by actions taken, even if the contract is not written or spoken.

Impound Account - A more formal term for the escrow account.

Improvement - Any alterations to or development of raw land. Improvement to raw land includes subdivision, installation of utilities, construction of buildings, landscaping and preparation for construction.

Improvement to Land - A specific group of publicly owned improvements that are meant to prepare raw land for further development. These improvements include curbs, streets, lights, sewers and sidewalks.

In-Law Unit - A semi-separate unit in a single-family residence or two-unit property. These added units were meant to provide separate living quarters for relatives, namely parents of the owners. These properties are often allowed exemptions to zoning laws that restrict residential buildings to single-family homes and prohibit multi-unit buildings.

Income - Money received from the investment of labor or capital. For standard mortgage purposes, the application must demonstrate sufficient income to qualify for the projected loan payments.

Income & Expense Statement - A summary of a company's or business' operating income and expenses for a given period. The employee can then use this W-2 to complete his or her tax returns, as well as maintain documentation of employment and income.

Income Approach to Property Value - The appraisal method is used to determine the value of a property, based on the revenue generated by the property. The gross rent multiplier (GRM) is calculated, based on the gross rent and market value of comparable rental properties. The gross rent from the subject property is then multiplied by the GRM to determine the property's market value, via the income approach. For example, if an appraiser is analyzing a four-flat and discovers that similar four-flats in the area have market values that are 10.5 times their market rents, the appraiser will use a GRM of 105. Applied to the subject property, the appraiser will multiply the subject property's market rental income by 10.5 to estimate the property's appraised value, via the income approach.

Income Property - Real estate property capable of producing rental revenue. Residential income property are any one-to-four unit, purely residential properties that can be leased out for rental income. Commercial income property include office complexes, commercial strip malls and apartment buildings.

Income Qualification - The analysis of an applicant's income to determine whether it is qualified, according to mortgage lender's guidelines, for a particular loan program. The lender normally qualifies the applicant's income by determining the debt-to-income (DTI) ratio and comparing that against the maximum ratios allowed for the particular loan program.

Income Qualification Worksheet - The calculation worksheet used to determine whether applicants meet conforming debt-to-income ratio guidelines.

Income Ratio - The percentage limits used to qualify the applicant's income, so as to determine whether the applicant can afford the loan. See the

Debt-to-Income Ratio entry.

Income Tax - A tax assessed by the government against individuals, based on that person's taxable income.

Incorporeal Interest - A non-possession right to real estate property.

Incurable Depreciation - Defects to a property that cannot be corrected or is not financially practical to correct. Unlike curable depreciation , incurable depreciation would entail diminishing returns, costs would exceed any projected increase in value.

Indemnification Letter, Affidavit - See Hold Harmless Letter entry.

Indemnify - To agree to hold a person or party free of liability. The person issuing the indemnification guarantee accepts all obligations for any liabilities that may arise from the agreed subject. For example, a refinance may discover a problem with the title that should have been addressed by the purchasing title company. The lender or title company for the refinance may require a "hold harmless" or indemnification letter from the original title insurer before the refinance can be closed.

Independent Contractor - A self-employed contractor, who provides services to a client on a contract or per project basis.

Index - For ARM loans, the index is the mechanism of economic measurements according to which ARM loan interest rates are adjusted. The most common ARM indices are the Treasury Bills, Cost of Funds Index (COFI), London InterBank Offered Rate (LIBOR) and Prime Rate.

Indexed Lease - A type of variable lease arrangement whose rental rates periodically adjust, based on the movement of a defined index. Many such index leases are based on the CPI or another industry standard index. Compare with graduated leases.

Index Method - A method used to estimate construction, reproduction and replacement costs that uses an index measuring the increase in construction costs for the subject's area. That index rate is then multiplied by the original cost of the subject property. Other methods include the square foot, cubic foot, unit in place and quantity survey methods.

Indexed Rate - With ARM loans, the indexed rate is the interest rate calculated by adding the program's (constant, fixed) margin to the (fluctuating) index.

Inducement - Elements in a contract that are provided for the benefit of the buyer or tenant, in order to persuade that buyer or tenant to sign the contract.

Industrial Development Bond - A bond instrument used to raise funds, which in turn are used to finance the development of an industrial facility. This bond is issued by the local or state government, provides certain tax advantages and is backed by the issuing government.

Industrial Park - An area usually designated for, consisting of or capable of hosting industrial facilities. The industrial park is usually designed to provide the utilities and amenities required to support industrial operations.

Industrial Property - Term used for commercial real estate directly involved in manufacturing, assembly or processing of goods and commodities. These properties include steel mills, assembly plants and small welding shops.

Infestation - Contamination of a property by pests. Although mice, rats and other wild animals are obnoxious and potentially unhealthy pests, the most dangerous pests--in the eyes of the real estate industry--are those that severely damage the home. The most dangerous pests are termites, carpenter ants and, to a lesser extent, powder post beetles. Many mortgage lenders refuse to close a loan unless such infestation problems are completely corrected.

Inflation - A persistent increase in price or a persistent decline in the purchasing power of money. Mortgage interest rates are normally tied to current trends or forecasts of inflation. As inflation or fear of potential inflation increases, interest rates also often rise. Inflation is measured and reported by the consumer price index (CPI) and producer price index (PPI).

Inner City - An imprecise term generally referring to the older portions of a city, outside of the central business district. The term is often used to indicate lower income areas of the city.

Inquiry (Credit) - A recorded request for a credit report. When an institution or other party orders a credit report on an applicant, the consumer's permanent history will record an inquiry, which identifies the party making the inquiry. section.

Inspection (Professional Property) - An investigation and analysis of a property by a qualified property inspector or engineer. Such inspections are optional but highly recommended for homebuyers.

Inspection Contingency - A common element of many residential sales contract that makes the agreement conditional upon the results of specific inspections, such as for termites, septic systems, structural stability and mechanical systems.

Inspection Fee - The charge levied by the lender to send an inspector to the subject property. This fee is normally associated with construction and rehab loans. The lender inspection is not the appraisal, nor is it the applicant-ordered inspection. Instead, the lender's inspection is commonly used to verify that the property is being completed according to the plans presented to and approved by the lender for the mortgage financing. Remember that construction loans are released in stages; the inspection fee usually covers the inspection that must be done as each stage is completed—so as to release the funds for the next step.

Inspection Period - The limited amount of time specified by the purchase agreement for buyer inspection of the property. This provision allows the buyer to requests amendments to the purchase agreement if serious defects are found by the inspection. If compensation for or repair of the defects is not provided by the seller, the buyer may terminate the agreement.

Installment Contract - An agreement between the buyer and the seller, which allows the buyer to purchase the property on installment. The seller, in fact, becomes the lender for the buyer's purchase. However, the property remains in the seller's name until the established price is fully paid. With an installment contract, the buyer is allowed to move in; the buyer pays monthly payments. Most installment contracts are essentially balloon in structure, giving the buyer a limited amount of time to eventually procure mortgage refinancing.

Installment Debt, Loan - A loan with a set starting balance that is paid off with constant periodic payments. Student, car and mortgage loans are essentially installment loans, in that it begins with a set principal balance and are paid off with periodic installment payments. By contrast, most credit cards are considered revolving accounts.

Installment Sale - A sales transaction that arranges for the proceeds to be paid in installments, so as to minimize any capital gains charges. Unlike the installment contract, the installment sale is a completed sales transaction with full transfer of ownership rights. The disbursements to the seller are simply delayed for tax purposes.

Instrument - A legal document that establishes certain rights, obligations and interests for the individuals or entities involved in the agreement.

Insulation - Protective material used in buildings to keep external heat or cold from entering, while also preventing internal cold or heat from escaping the building. The four most common types of insulation are blanket, loose-fill, sheet and reflective. All insulation are graded by their R-value.

Insurance - A legal agreement in which the insurer agrees to compensate the insured individual or entity for specifically covered losses incurred by the insured party. The insurance coverage is provided in exchange for specified premiums.

Insured Loan - A loan insured either by the FHA, VA or by a private mortgage insurance (PMI) company.

Inter Vivos Trust - See Living Trust entry.

Interest – The cost of using someone else's money. The interest is usually expressed as an annual interest rate, which is then applied to the loan principal balance.

Interest-Only Balloon, Loan - A balloon loan in which only the interest is paid during the term; the payment schedule does NOT make any arrangements for the reduction of the principal balance. However, the borrower is free to make additional payments for the purpose of reducing the principal. At the end of the balloon term, the principal balance must be paid. Many home equity lines of credit (HELOC) are interest-only loan programs.

Interest Rate - The cost of using someone else's money, as expressed as a percentage relative to the amount of the loan principal balance.

Interim Loan, Interim Financing - A short-term loan (often used in construction) made with the expectation of repayment from the proceeds of another loan. For example, a construction loan is usually a short-term loan used to fund the actual construction of the subject property. As soon as the construction is complete, the construction loan must be refinanced with a standard long-term loan.

Interior Partitions - Any non-bearing wall or partition that enclose or subdivide the open spaces within a building.

Intermediary Theory - Also called modified lien theory, this system is used by some states, which combine both the title theory and lien theory systems. In the intermediary system, the title remains with the mortgagor. However, if the mortgagor defaults on the loan, the mortgagee may quickly take full possession.

Internal Rate of Return - The rate of return on the investment. The specific definition of the IRR is the discounted rate that produces a zero value for the net present value.

Internal Revenue Code - The federal laws that regulate income taxes.

Intestate - An individual who or the situation in which an individual dies without a valid will.

Inventory - Any property held by an individual or entity for future sale or use.

Inverse Condemnation - A legal remedy for property owners facing eminent domain proceedings. If the government exercises its eminent domain powers and begins condemnation proceedings to take a piece of a landowner's property, that landowner may force the government to take the entire property.

Inverted Yield Curve - An occasional, but rare situation in which the yield curve (going from short-term to long-term) slopes downward-- rather than upward.

Investment Property - In the residential mortgage industry, an investment property is any real estate that is NOT occupied by the borrower and is owned for the purpose of generating supplemental income. Note that the residential market distinguishes between three types of properties: primary (owner-occupied), secondary (vacation) or investment properties.

Investment Tax Credit - A reduction in income tax based on the cost and life of certain purchased assets.

Investment Value of Equity - A discounted cash flow technique that values after-tax cash flow and after-tax equity reversion.

Investor - Within the mortgage origination industry, the investor is the funding source of the lender's mortgage funds. If a mortgage broker sells to or originates for a specific bank, then that institution is the investor for the mortgage broker.

Investor Note Financing - The financing of investor promissory notes.

Involuntary Alienation - Legal term describing the transfer of title to property without the current owner's consent. Such involuntary transfers typically occur through descent, eminent domain, lien foreclosure , escheat, adverse possession and accession.

Involuntary Lien - Any claim or lien legally recorded against a property without the previous consent of the owner. The most common of such liens are for real estate taxes and judgments. Compare with voluntary lien.

Irrevocable Trust - A type of living trust that cannot be changed once they are created. Compare with revocable trusts.

J-L

| Jalousie Window - See Louver Window entry.

Jambs - Construction term referring to the sides of the frame in which windows are installed. The head jamb is the top part of the window frame, while side jambs are the side panels of the typical window frame. For more information about the parts and styles of windows, see the Windows entry.

Joint and Several Liability - Legal term applying full obligation to repay a debt on each of the multiple borrowers of the debt. Each of the borrowers is fully liable for payment of the debt. Liability is NOT proportional to ownership interest.

Joint Tenancy With Right of Survivorship - An ownership of property arrangement by two or more parties. If a joint tenant dies, his or her interest does not necessarily pass on to an heir. Instead, the ownership of the property is shared by the remaining, surviving joint tenants. In states where this is an acceptable form of ownership, this avoids probate problems. Compare with Tenants in Common, Community Property or Tenants by Entirety. Note, however, that the co-owners have divided ownership of the property and can sell such ownership shares; but such a sale would keep the joint tenancy between the remaining original joint tenants. The new co-owner would have a tenants in common relationship with the remaining original co-owners.

Joint Venture - An agreement between two or more parties to cooperate on a project. Unlike a partnership, the parties remain separate--although they may have varying levels of responsibilities for portions of the project. Joint ventures are usually intended for a limited duration and are dissolved once the project is complete.

Joist - Horizontal planks, usually 2x6 or 2x8 in size, that create a load-bearing frame for the floor and ceilings. Joists are normally laid across the shortest house dimension. Joist spans that are more than 16 feet in length normally use girders for additional support.

Judgment - A legal finding by a judge or court of law. A judgment can sometimes force garnishment of wages or assets to satisfy the judgment debt. In terms of credit, judgments are unsecured liens filed against a person for non- payment of debt. With most debts (installment loans, credit card balances, medical bills, etc.), if the consumer fails to make payments, the lender will pursue the borrower with delinquency notices, default notices, collection and, if the balance is large enough, a legal judgment.

Judgment Affidavit - A legal form that identifies any and all judgments against the person or institution providing the affidavit. Many closing agents will require a judgment affidavit from the borrower at the time of closing to ensure that all potentially encumbering judgments are identified.

Judgment Lien - A claim on a person's property that arises from a court-ordered judgment against that person or entity. During the judgment process, the court may issue a writ of attachment to prohibit transfer of property and a writ of execution to seize the property.

Judicial foreclosure - Also called foreclosure by sale, this type of foreclosure uses the courts to take the title of the collateral property away from the mortgagor. The two most common types of judicial foreclosures are judicial sales and strict foreclosures.

Judicial Sale - An involuntary sale of a property ordered by the court, usually after a judgment arising from a foreclosure. Unlike a strict foreclosure , this process has the court order a sale of the property to the highest bidder. The proceeds are used to satisfy the lien holders, with any remnants going to the mortgagor.

Jumbo Loan - A non-conforming loan with an amount higher than the maximum loan amounts accepted by FNMA or FHLMC. As of 2001, the maximum loan amounts accepted by Fannie Mae and Freddie Mac are $275,00 for single-unit homes and $528,700 for four-unit residential properties.

Junior Mortgage - Any mortgage claim whose lien is lower in priority than other mortgage liens. Home equity loans, second mortgage and, when applicable, third mortgages are considered junior liens to the first mortgage. If the property is ever sold, the proceeds must first satisfy tax and primary liens; the remaining surplus is then used to satisfy

junior mortgages.

Kickboard - See Base Molding entry.

Kicker - Real estate term referring to additional interest or rent payments that may be required by a contract.

Kiln Dried - Lumber seasoned in a temperature- and humidity-controlled oven to minimize shrinkage and warping.

Lally Column - A big steel pipe sometimes filled with concrete and used to support girders or beams.

Land - The surface of the earth that is not water. In the real estate industry, land encompasses the earth's surface and natural entities permanently attached to that parcel of land, as well as the air space above and minerals and soil below.

Land Banking - The investment tactic of purchasing land that will be held for future use or needs.

Land Contract - A more common term for an installment purchase agreement.

Land Lease - An arrangement by which land is leased. A buyer can purchase a building separately from the land upon which that structure is located. The building is bought in the standard way, but the buyer can simply lease the land. This lowers the overall price, and the seller lowers potential capital gains .

Land Loan - Funds loaned for the purchase or refinance of raw land—without the improvements to be built or currently on that property. For example, home buyers seeking to construct their own home will first purchase the land, then proceed with trying to procure construction financing and contractors.

Land Packaging - The process of combining multiple parcels of property (usually raw or minimally developed) into one large parcel for a specific use.

Land Sale Leaseback - An agreement in which the current owners of a land sells a parcel of property (usually raw or minimally developed), but then leases that land from the new owner.

Land Trust - A type of trust in which the only asset is the real estate, and legal title to the property is held by the trustee. A deed in trust is used to transfer real estate into the trust; and a trustee's deed is required to take the property out of trust. Land trusts are typically for a fixed term, usually 20 years, but can be extended. Land trusts provide privacy, because only the trustee's name is recorded. Because the beneficiary's interest in the land trust is considered personal property, it also simplifies transfer of ownership, avoids transfer taxes, limits personal liability and protects from encumbrances.

Landlocked - A condition in which a parcel of property has no access to a public street, thoroughfare or right of way.

Landlord, Landlady - Term applied for owner of a rental property. As with many American real estate terms, this term comes from Old English title for landowners.

Lap Joint - A connection made by placing two pieces of material side by side and then nailed or glued together.

Lath - Thin, narrow strips of wood often used to set a base for slates, tiles or plastering.

Late Charge - Any fee added to an installment as a penalty for not meeting a payment deadline. Most residential loan lenders will provide a 10- to 15-

day grace period after the due date before a late charge is assessed.

Latent Defects - Any deficiencies that are currently not visible or existing, but will arise or appear in the future.

Lead - Soft metallic element found in rocks and soil that had been widely used in plumbing, paints and fuel until the 1980s. High concentration can damage the brain, nervous system and other organs. Many states require sellers to disclose lead content to buyer prior to purchase.

Lead-Based Paint Hazard & Reduction Act - This federal legislation affecting pre-1978 residential properties requires owners to provide written disclosures to lessees and buyers of the existence of lead-based paint.

Lease, Lease Agreement - An agreement in which an individual or corporation may receive possession, or temporary ownership, of real property for a specific period of time. Strictly speaking, when a property owner offers a lease, he or she is agreeing to a voluntary alienation of the property for the specified period. A lease agreement transfers the right of possession to the tenant, but the landlord retains reversion rights.

Lease with Purchase Option - A lease agreement that provides the renter with a limited right to buy a property, usually available within a specified time frame with predefined conditions.

Leasehold, Leasehold Estate - A form of property ownership that provides for only temporary ownership. In contrast to freehold estates, leasehold estates is of limited duration, have fewer property ownership rights and is usually created with a lease agreement. There are four basic types of leasehold estates: estate for years, periodic estate, tenancy at will and tenancy at sufferance.

Leasehold Mortgage - A mortgage lien applied against a tenant's ownership interest in a property.

Leasehold Policy - A type of title insurance policy that assures renters that they have a valid lease from the owner.

Leasing Agent - The individual responsible for the marketing of rental space.

Legal Description of Property - The precise survey description of the property used for recording exact property location and size. The legal title to a property will use this legal description, which will fully distinguish the property from any other plot of land in the nation, if not the world. Most descriptions employ a combination of at least two of the three types of surveying systems: metes and bounds, rectangular survey system and plat of survey methods.

Legal Life Estate - One of two types of non-inheritable or life estates, this legal real estate term applies to life estates created by law or legislation. There are three common forms—dower, curtesy and homestead estates-- but not all states recognize all three.

Legal Name - The name used for official purposes to identify a person or entity.

Legal Notice - A formal, legally recognized announcement or notification that is given to another person or entity.

Legatee - An individual or entity who receives any property through a will.

Lender - The person or institution who provides money to a borrower for a limited period in exchange for full repayment of the original principal loan balance plus loan costs. Mortgage documents often refer to the lender as the mortgagee.

Lender Subsidy - Any contributions made by the lender to cover any portion of the borrower's closing costs. Lenders are often allowed to cover the borrower's closing costs. However, there are normally restrictions on the lender's subsidy.

Lender's title insurance Policy - Also called a mortgagee's policy, a type of title insurance policy that protects lenders against both known and latent title defects that could affect its ability to adequately secure its mortgage loan. It only covers the loan amount. Unlike other title policies, the lender's policy is assignable and has no exceptions for claims that could have been discovered with a physical inspection of the subject property.

Lessee - In a lease arrangement, the party that rents and will occupy the property.

Lessor - In a lease agreement, the landowner or party leasing out the property to another party.

Letter of Intent - A written expression of an individual's or entity's intention to enter into an agreement or perform an action. This letter is usually non-binding and dependent on other conditions.

Level Payment Mortgage - A mortgage loan program that imposes the same payment amount on the borrower for the entire term of the loan. The popular 30-year fixed-rate program is the most obvious example of a level payment mortgage program.

Leverage - The capacity to borrow money against the property's equity; the larger the loan in relation to the equity, the greater that the property is leveraged. For example, a $100,000 home with only $10,000 in mortgage liens is considered lightly leveraged, while a similar $100,000 home with $95,000 in mortgage liens is considered heavily leveraged. If that same property had $125,000 in mortgage liens, it would be considered over-leveraged.

Levy - The process of assessing a tax upon a person, property or entity.

Liabilty - The borrower's obligations to repay creditors or lenders.

Liability Insurance, Coverage - A form of insurance coverage for a property that reimburses the insured entity for claims arising from specified physical damages to the property or injuries incurred by persons on or because of the property and the owner's negligence.

License - In the real estate industry, a license is a right to use a property for a defined period, usually for a specific purpose. Licenses are normally non-transferrable. Unlike a lease, the license does not transfer any ownership rights. For example, Gina may allow her brother Leo to use her home as collateral for his business loan. She still completely owns the property and she won't sign the business loan note (except for the mortgage deed); rather she simply permits her brother to use her property in a certain way.

Lien - A legal claim or attachment, filed on record, against a property. This lien is usually a security for the payment of an obligation. If the collateral property is foreclosed and sold, the proceeds would first go toward fully satisfying The first or priority lien debts, before attempting to repay any secondary liens. Liens can be specific or general, voluntary or involuntary, and contractual, statuary or equitable.

Lien Holder - Any person, government entity, lender, creditor or institution who has a recorded lien on a property.

Lien Theory - A system used by most states, which practice that a mortgage does not give ownership to the mortgagee (lender). The mortgage only files a lien against the property, but the title remains with the mortgagor. If the mortgagor defaults on the loan, the mortgagee must foreclose on the owner to take possession. However, the defeasance clause reverts the title back to the mortgagor as soon as the loan is paid. Other states follow the title theory and intermediary theory systems.

Life Estate - An individual's or entity's freehold interest in a property, which will expire upon the death of the owner or another specified person. See Conventional Life Estate entry.

Life Tenant - An individual or entity who is permitted to occupy or use a property until the death of that individual or another specified person.

Like Property, Like-Kind Property - Properties that have the same nature or usage that are used in a property exchange. For more information, see the Real Estate Exchange entry.

Limited Documentation Loan - A limited documentation or "lite doc" loan accept alternative documentation for certain processing requirements. For example, a limited documentation program would accept the average monthly deposits from bank statements as documentation of income, in lieu of pay stubs normally required.

Limited Liability - A type of liability that limits the investor's obligation to the amount invested by the investor.

Limited Liability Company (LLC) - A variation of a corporate business structure that provides the investor with the legal protection and organization of a corporation, while offering some of the tax benefits of a partnership or subchapter-S corporation. LLC owners are called members; they have limited liability and avoid the double taxation of corporations.

LLCs are ideal for small, closely held companies.

Limited Partners - Passive investors in a limited partnership. The liability obligation of limited partners is limited to the amount they have invested.

Limited Partnership - A type of partnership that caps the partner's liability, but also limits the partner's control. A limited partnership must have at least one general partner to manage the project. The partnership liability of limited partners are only limited to his or her investment.

Limited Warranty Deed - A type of deed of conveyance that provides the grantee with a lesser degree of grantor assurances than the General Warranty Deed.

Line of Credit - A financing option that provides a credit line instead of a lump-sum loan, from which the borrower may quickly and randomly borrow. See the Home Equity Line of Credit entry.

Lintel - The top piece above a door or window that supports the wall above the opening.

Liquid Asset - Cash, or any other assets that may be easily and quickly converted to cash. Stocks, bonds, certificates of deposits and most securities are considered liquid assets because they can be quickly sold for cash.

Liquidated Damages - Funds or moneys identified as compensation amount to be paid if one of the parties to a contract breaches elements of the contract.

Liquidity - The ease and speed by which assets held in other forms can be converted into cash.

Lis Pendens - A legal term basically meaning that a suit may be pending. When real estate is involved, the plaintiff may record a lis pendens to publicly warn all potential purchasers that the subject property is subject to a possible judgment.

List Price - The current asking price advertised in a property listing.

Listed Property - Properties sold through real estate agents are normally "listed" by seller's agent as for sale. Affiliated real estate agencies will list their for-sale properties with a multiple listing service to broadly advertise their listings.

Listing Agent - A real estate agent who is responsible for selling a property. The seller's agent will list the property as "for sale" within the office and with a local multiple listing service.

Listing Agreement - A contract between a seller and an agent, in which the agent is hired to find a ready, willing and able buyer for the seller's property.

Littoral Rights - Legal concept concerning water rights for property owners whose land abuts a lake, ocean, sea or other non- flowing bodies of water. Property ownership of land extends to the high-water mark at the water's edge.

Living Trust - Sometimes called an Inter Vivos trust, a type of trust created by the owner of the subject property during the lifetime of that owner. The two basic types of living trusts are the Irrevocable trust and the Revocable trust. The

chief advantages of the living trust are that they provide for automatic transfer of property upon death of the owner while avoiding the cost and delay of probate.

LLC - See Limited Liability Company entry.

Load Factor - Space in a rental building that does not produce rental income. Hallways, maintenance closets and lobby areas are a load against the owner, since they don't generate income—although the owner is still responsible for their upkeep and maintenance. The load factor is often indicated as a percentage of the total rentable area of the property.

Loan - The granting of the use of money, in return for the money's return along with interest.

Loan Broker - A financing professional who arranges loans between clients and lenders. For more information, see Mortgage Broker entry.

Loan Commitment - A written commitment from the lender that the application has been fully approved and that the loan transaction may be closed. The commitment may include closing conditions and will have a set duration.

Loan Constant - Any factor or multiplier that is used to compute the periodic interest or P&I payments on a loan.

Loan Officer - The lender's representative who is responsible for beginning and facilitating the loan application process.

Loan Poolers - Private institutions that purchase loans that will be securitized and sold to the secondary mortgage market, in cooperation with Ginnie Mae.

Loan Processor - The lender's representative who is responsible for verifying and documenting the loan application data, as well as assisting the loan officer and underwriter in facilitating the loan's closing.

Loan-To-Value (LTV) Ratio - The ratio of the loan amount in relation to the appraised value of the property. For example, an $80,000 loan ($20,000 down payment) on a $100,000 property constitutes an 80% LTV. Most lenders express their exposure for specific programs in terms of LTV limits. For example, most conforming lenders limit their exposure on the purchases of single-family homes to 95% LTV, which means that the borrower must provide at least a 5% down payment.

Location - The site or placement of an entity. In real estate, location often refers to the relative advantages of one site, because of any amenities, attractiveness and social factors associated with that site.

Location Note Endorsement - The guarantee issued by the title search company or attorney that verifies the true and precise location of the property, in reference to the legal description, recorded survey and/or common street address. With refinances, a location note endorsement can be used and is preferable to the much more expensive survey.

Lock (Loan) - A loan registration with a lender that instructs the lender to set aside a certain amount of money for the borrower, at a specified interest rate. When the rate is locked, both the lender and the borrower are committed to closing and disbursing the loan with that interest rate—within the lock period.

Lock Period - The length of time for which the loan rate lock will remain in effect. Typically, the longer the lock period requested, the higher the cost for the borrower in terms of interest rate or origination, discount or commitment fees.

Loft - A building unit, usually an apartment, townhouse or condominium, in which interior walls are minimized to provide a roomier, more open space. In most lofts, interior walls do not reach all the way to the ceiling.

Long-Term Capital Gain - An income tax designation referring to gains received from the sale of capital assets that have been held by the property owner for an IRS- or industry-specified period of time.

Long-Term Debt, Liabilities - Liabilities that will take at least 10 months to repay. When qualifying an applicant's income, the lender will consider the total long-term debt payments as a ratio against the applicant's gross income. Installment loans normally have set monthly payments that are used for the income qualification ratios. Except for very low balances, most revolving accounts are qualified based on the minimum required monthly payment at the time of application.

Long-Term Debt Ratio - See Back-End Ratio entry.

Loose Fill Insulation - A type of insulation material commonly used to fill wall cavities and flat areas above ceilings in homes. As the name implies, loose fill insulation normally consists of pebble-sized material that is blown unto and allowed to settle in target areas. The most common types of loose fill material are fiberglass, rock wool, cellulose fiber, vermiculite and perlite. For more information about types of insulation, see the Insulation entry.

Loss Assessment Insurance - Insurance against the policyholder being assessed by his or her homeowners association due to a loss suffered by the homeowners association, which exceeds the association's insurance limits.

Lot and Block, Lot-Block-Tract Method - A method of property identification that is often used in urban and developed areas. See the Plat of Survey System entry.

Louver Window - A type of window that consists of overlapping horizontal glass louvers (slats) that are opened and closed together with a lever or crank. It can provide excellent weather protection and ventilation. Unfortunately, louver windows may not always be able to provide a perfect seal. For more information about the parts and styles of windows, see the Windows entry.

Low Emissivity Glass - Sometimes called low-E glass, this is a type of glass that allows certain wavelengths of light through it, while reflecting other wavelengths. This has the effect of reducing the transfer of heat, allowing low-E glass to block ultraviolet rays and summer heat, while trapping winter sunlight. For more information about the parts and styles of windows, see the Windows entry.

Low-Rise - Any building containing up to three stories (not including the basement).

Lower Chord - Construction term referring to the beam that connects the bottom ends of rafters in a truss roof frame. With the two sloping rafters, the horizontal lower chord creates a triangular frame used to support the roof. The lower chord may be connected to the rafter with bolts or a gusset plate.

M

Maintenance - The process of or actions required to repair or prevent normal wear and tear incurred by a property.

Maintenance Fee - Among property owner's associations, this fee is a charge to cover the cost of maintaining or operating a property.

Mall - A mall may be an open plaza-like area, but is more often a term referring to an area connecting retail stores in a retail center.

Management Contract - A formal agreement between a property owner and a management company.

Managing Partner - In a limited partnership, the partner who makes the decisions and bears the largest portion of the partnership's risk.

Mansard Roof - A type of roof design that contains two slopes on each of the four sides. The mansard roof normally has no gables and contains eight slopes in all. The top of the mansard roof often looks like an "X" as intersecting ridge lines are set from corner to opposite corner. The intersection at the middle is the highest point. The upper slopes normally do not have a steep incline. By contrast, the lower slopes on each side are so steep that they are almost vertical.

Manufactured Home - A property primarily produced in a factory or similar manufacturing facility and subsequently assembled at the home site. Most consumers identify manufactured homes as mobile home or trailer homes, but the manufactured home industry is now more diverse. There are now basically four types of manufactured homes: mobile, modular, panelized and pre-cut.

Map Book - See the Plat Book entry.

Margin (ARM) - Used with adjustable-rate mortgage (ARM) loans when calculating periodic interest rate adjustments. When the ARM rate is adjusted, the margin is the additional constant rate added to the index rate to calculate the new ARM rate. The margin is established and fixed at the beginning of the loan, in the promissory note. For example, a conforming Treasury Bill ARM reaches its one-year anniversary. Its margin is 3.00, as established in the original promissory note. At the time of the rate adjustment, the average T-Bill index rate has been calculated at 4.250%. The margin is added to the T-Bill index for a new rate of 7.250%; however, this is subject to the periodic and lifetime caps applicable with the specific ARM program.

Margin Loan - Funds borrowed against a person's current deposits or investment balance. Financial institutions often allow their individual investors to borrow against the value of their individual portfolios, up to a percentage of their portfolio value--usually 50%. A drop in the stock market may lower the portfolio value, which would increase the ratio of margin loan. It if exceeds the limit, "margin calls" are made and private investors must immediately pay down their loan to bring it within limits.

Marginal Property - Any property capable of producing only very low economic return, or any property approaching full economic and functional obsolescence.

Marginal Tax Rate - The income tax rate incurred by the last dollar of a person's or entity's income.

Market Allocation - A violation of federal antitrust laws in which competitors avoid or eliminate direct competition by agreeing to divide the market into exclusive areas.

Market Analysis - A review and study of the impact of economic (supply &

demand) forces on an investment property.

Market Approach - See Comparative Market Approach entry.

Market Rent - The rental rate for a subject property's rental units, based on the rents of units in comparable properties in the same area.

Market Research - The investigation and study conducted to determine the market conditions in an area or the impact of a certain product in a market.

Market Risk - The probability of an investment's failure that may be caused by external market conditions.

Market Value, Fair Market Value - The highest price that is the most probable point at which the willing, unrelated, competent and able buyer and seller will freely agree. The appraisal attempts to calculate the estimated fair market value of the subject property through recent market sales comparisons, cost-to-rebuild and, when applicable, income approaches.

Marketable Title - A title that contains no major defects that may prohibit the sale or transfer of the title.

Marketing Time - The amount of time required to sell an item. In the real estate industry, marketing time is normally applied to the average time from the moment the property is listed for sale and the moment that a purchase contract is signed.

Master Deed - See Declaration of Condominium entry.

Master Lease - A lease that allows the renter (master lessee) to relet the property to other renters. The master lessee is responsible for management and marketing the properties. Typically, the owner or master lessor is guaranteed a regular installment regardless of how well the master lessee is performing. The master lessee (renter) assumes all of the risk; however, the owner (master lessor) receives much less than if he or she were to manage the property directly.

Master Plan - The growth map created and maintained by a community to chart overall development plan for the community. The master plan will include zoning restrictions and establish development priorities.

Mattress Money - A casual term used for funds or assets that are undocumented, as in money saved in a person's mattress or hidden coffee can. Most conforming loan programs will not accept undocumented funds, when underwriting the applicant for a mortgage loan. However, some nonconforming loans do accept undocumented funds through No Documentation and No Asset Verification (NAV) programs.

Maturity - The date at which a loan's final payment is due. With a 30-year fixed-rate loan, the loan's maturity is the end of the term (360th month); with a five-year balloon, the loan matures at the end of the fifth year.

Mechanic's Lien - Also know as "mechanic's and materialmen's (M&M) lien," this is a claim for payment of services or materials furnished. For example, when construction or rehab work is completed (or materials for such provided) but unpaid, the contractors may place a lien against the property until the amount due is fully paid.

Merchant's Association - An organization of retail merchants in a shopping center or district. Much like a chamber of commerce, the members of a merchant's association promote the business success of its members.

Meridian - A circular line that passes through both global poles. The term is sometimes used in real estate surveys to delineate a north-south line of reference. See also the Principal Meridian entry.

Metes - In the metes and bounds system of surveying, metes refer to the distance measurements used to describe the boundaries of a parcel of property.

Metes and bounds - One of the oldest established method of surveying property is the metes and bounds system. This system describes the boundaries of properties through metes (distance) and bounds (direction) starting and eventually ending at a point of beginning. However, this normally produces lengthy and complicated descriptions and POB monuments can often be altered. Compare with Rectangular Survey System and Plat of Survey methods.

Millage - A property tax rate used to calculate a parcel's tax assessment. One mill is equal to 1/1000 of a dollar, or 1/10 of one cent.

Mineral Rights - Property rights involving ownership and disposition of minerals and other subsurface natural resources.

Mini-Warehouse - A prevalent type of warehouse that provides smaller storage spaces for residential and commercial users.

MIP - See Mortgage Insurance Premium entry.

Mirror Image Offer - In the real estate market, any offer from a prospective offer that satisfies the terms of the listing contract. If the seller rejects such an offer, the agent is often still entitled to a compensation.

Mixed-Use Project - A planned development intended to include space for different types of real estate usage.

Mixed-use Property - A multiple-unit property which contains both residential and commercial units. Many older city buildings on major thoroughfares have commercial storefronts on the first floor and residential apartments on the upper floors.

Mobile Home - Often called a trailer home, mobile homes are the most complete and least expensive type of manufactured homes. Originally, mobile were trailers that could be pulled by a car or truck. Mobile homes today are no longer so mobile. They are much larger and no longer designed for lengthy road travel; they are normally semi-permanently anchored and connected to utilities.

Mobile Home Park - A type of land subdivision that allots a property for mobile homes.

Model Unit - An initial unit in a property development that is intended to provide a representative view of the planned units when completed. The model unit is a marketing tool used by developers to sell a non-completed unit to potential buyers by offering a example of the final appearance of the finished product.

Modification - Real estate terminology referring to an economic characteristic of real estate that changes to the land affects the value of the property.

Modified Lien Theory - See Intermediary Theory entry.

Modular Home - A type of manufactured home structure that produces entire sections of the home in the factory. The single-room or multi-room sections are then assembled at the site. Modular homes are normally at least twice the size of comparable mobile homes and often resemble smaller ranch-style housing.

Molding - See Trim entry.

Monolithic Slab - A type of foundation used in some structures, in which the foundation slab and walls are poured as one cohesive unit. This method is often used with garages and porches.

Month-to-Month Tenancy - A type of lease arrangement in which the tenant's interest in the leasehold property is renewed on a monthly basis for a one-month term. Either the landlord or tenant may terminate the lease arrangement at the conclusion of each month.

Monthly Payment - The amount due each period on a debt, whether installment or revolving. For mortgage purposes, this is the sum amount of the projected principal, interest, taxes and insurance (PITI) paid each month on a mortgage loan.

Mortgage - A conditional conveyance of property as security for a debt; to offer a property as a security for a loan. With a mortgage loan, the borrower will still own the property; the mortgage merely gives the lender the right to foreclose and obtain ownership if the borrower defaults on the loan.

Mortgage Backed Securities (MBS) - Securities sold in the financial markets and collateralized by multi-million dollar blocks of mortgage loans. MBS are the source for much of the funds for conforming loans.

Mortgage Banker - A bank that concentrates primarily in originating mortgage loans that will probably be sold in the secondary market. A mortgage banker may originate loans directly with borrowers or through brokers.

Mortgage Broker - an intermediary, between the borrower and a lender, responsible for arranging and packaging the loan application. The broker is usually the person or agency who originates mortgage loans with the funds of other correspondent lenders. Because mortgage brokers can and do work with an almost unlimited number of lending institutions, they offer more loan program options to most borrowers.

Mortgage Commitment - See Loan Commitment entry.

Mortgage Contingency - The clause in the real estate purchase contract that sets a deadline for buyer procurement of a mortgage loan commitment. The contingency date protects both the buyer and the seller. If the buyer is unable to obtain a mortgage loan commitment by this date, the seller can cancel the loan or provide an extension. If the buyer surpasses this contingency date without an extension and later fails to obtain a mortgage loan, then the seller can sometimes retain the earnest money deposit. See also Contingency Date entry.

Mortgage Correspondent - A person or entity who originates and services a loan.

Mortgage Deed, Note - A written description of the security for a promise to repay a debt. Separate and distinct from the promissory note, the mortgage deed or note is the instrument that actually offers the subject property as collateral for the loan.

Mortgage Insurance - Mortgage insurance, both government or privately issued, protect the lender by guaranteeing a portion of the loan amount against losses. For example, if a lender holds an $80,000 mortgage (with expenses) and sells a foreclosure home for only $75,000, the mortgage insurance would reimburse the lender for that $5,000 short-fall. FHA and VA loans are essentially mortgage insurance programs; conventional loans require private mortgage insurance (PMI). With conforming loans, mortgage insurance is required whenever the LTV ratio exceeds 80%.

Mortgage Insurance Premium (MIP) - The monthly premium paid by a borrower for mortgage insurance on FHA loans. Mortgage insurance is generally required for mortgage loans with LTV ratios in excess of 80%.

Mortgage Lien - A lien or encumbrance recorded against a property that is used to secure a mortgage loan obligation.

Mortgage Life Insurance - A form of credit life insurance that pays off the balance of the mortgage loan amount in the event of death or incapacitation of the insured borrower.

Mortgage Loan - A type of financing secured by a real estate mortgage deed. With mortgage loans, the borrower normally still owns the subject property. The mortgage deed offers the property as security and provides the lender with the right to foreclose the property if the loan defaults.

Mortgage REIT - One of two types of real estate investment trusts. The mortgage REIT invests in mortgage loans by lending mortgage loans for target properties.

Mortgage Release - A disclaimer granted by the lender releasing the borrower from any further liability on the mortgage. Once the mortgage loan balance is fully repaid or satisfied, the lender issues a mortgage release to remove any liens from the property.

Mortgagee - The lender of money in a mortgage transaction. In the mortgage loan context, the lender accepts the collateral property being offered by the mortgagor/borrower/mortgagor as security for the loan.

Mortgagee Clause - The formal term for the escrow clause normally included in the insurance certificate. The mortgagee clause identifies the lender.

Mortgagor - The person or entity mortgaging property for consideration. In current terms, the mortgagor is the person borrowing and receiving money from the lender in the mortgage transaction—and using personal property as security or collateral for a loan.

Mullion - The slender framing strips of material that divide the panes of a window.

Multi-Family Mortgage - Mortgage industry term for mortgage financing on any residential real estate property with five or more apartment units.

Multi-Unit Property - Strictly speaking, it is any property with two or more units. However, this terms is normally only used for residential properties with five or more apartment units.

Multiple Exchange - The most common type of real estate exchanges involves more than two parties, since it is very difficult to find two parties willing to swap properties directly. The Starker exchange is actually a variation of this approach.

Multiple Listing Service (MLS) - An MLS is a forum for sharing properties "listed" for sale among affiliated real estate brokers. Realtors and agents often form local and regional boards, which are normally responsible for maintaining an MLS that allows all affiliates to access information about current and recent listed properties. An MLS listing provides greater exposure for sellers and the broker's listing.

Muntins - Construction term referring to the strips in a window sash that separate the individual window panes. For more information about the parts and styles of windows, see the Windows entry.

WILLIAM E KEELER

N-O

Naked Title - Also called barely legal title, this is the type of title given to the trustee in a deed of trust. Instead of actual title, the trustee does not receive the same rights as standard ownership.

National Environmental Policy Act - A 1967 federal legislation that promoted efforts to reduce damage to the environment. Its most enduring legacy is environmental impact statements it required for new projects.

National Flood Insurance Program - Flood insurance assistance for property owners, created by Congress and managed by FEMA's Federal Insurance Administration. Homeowners can obtain flood insurance coverage if their community participates in NFIP flood control programs. In recent years, however, the federal government has curtailed flood insurance assistance, so as to discourage development in flood-prone areas.

National Housing Act - A 1934 legislation that established the Federal Housing Administration (FHA).

Negative Amortization - A situation in which the loan principal is actually increasing, instead of decreasing. This usually happens when the payments are less than the amount of the interest due, so that the overdue interest becomes part of the principal balance. Some ARM loans may incur negative amortization, because as caps are factored in, the capped payment is insufficient to cover the interest due. Thus, the unpaid or deferred interest becomes additional principal. F

Negative Cash Flow - With rental property, this situation occurs when rental income is not enough to cover operating and mortgage expenses. If an applicant has negative rental cash flow from any property owned, that rent loss must be listed as a long-term loss and included in the applicant's debt-to-income (DTI) ratio.

Negative Easement - A type of easement that prevents the owner from certain actions or uses. For example, one landowner may obtain an easement barring his neighbor from building something so tall that it would block the sunlight. Compare this to positive easement.

Negative Net Worth - The financial situation wherein a person's total liabilities exceeds total assets. Persons with a heavy burden of student and other unsecured loans often suffer from this dilemma. Lenders look unfavorably upon negative or weak net worth; applicants should include additional properties in the asset section to offset liabilities.

Neighborhood - A primarily contiguous area, usually in urban or developed settings, whose occupants have established a community of interactive relationships.

 Neighborhood Shopping Center - A small retail center or mall, usually anchored by a supermarket, pharmacy or department store. The typical size for neighborhood shopping centers is about 100,000 square feet.

Net Income - Portion of gross income remaining after taxes and deductions. For consumers, it is essentially their take-home pay. For income properties, it is gross income less operating expenses.

Net Leasable Area - The total floor space that is actually leased to a tenant, per the lease agreement.

Net Lease - A lease arrangement that assesses the tenant with a base rent plus an additional assessment for the tenant's share of building operating expenses (CAM), insurance or real estate taxes. Net leases are either Single-Net,

Double-Net (NN) or Triple-Net (NNN), depending on the number of expenses (CAM, insurance or taxes) that the lessee must pay.

Net Listing - A type of listing agreement in which the seller has indicated the amount he or she is seeking; the broker's commission will be the difference between the sales price and that seller-indicated target. This is an illegal format in many states, because of the potential for fraud.

Net Net Lease - See Double Net Lease entry.

Net Net Net Lease - See Triple Net Lease entry.

Net Operating Income - The income amount remaining after all operating expenses have been paid.

Net Operating Income Multiplier - A measurement of a property investment's rate of return. This calculation is the net operating income divided by the property's sale price. It is essentially the inverse of the overall capitalization rate.

Net Present Value - The present value of an investment's projected income less the present value of the investment's projected expenses.

Net Rental Income - The portion of the gross rental income remaining after operating expenses and mortgage payments are paid.

Net Worth - Total assets minus total liabilities. If liabilities exceed assets, the borrower would have a negative net worth, which would jeopardize loan application qualifications.

NNN - See Triple Net Lease entry.

No Asset Verification (NAV) Loan - A non-conforming loan program that requires no documentation of the qualifying asset's source. However, the existence of the assets or funds in question must still be verified. For example, an applicant with mattress money or undocumented funds may use this program. The applicant merely needs to show that the funds for the down payment and closing exist; however, there is no need to document the source of the funds.

No Closing Cost Program - A loan program in which the borrower is not charged any closing costs. Most of these programs still charge closing costs, but the borrower does not have to pay them out of pocket. Instead, the closing costs are financed through the loan in one way or another.

No Documentation (No Doc) Loan - The No Doc loan is usually a combination of the No Asset Verification (NAV) and No Income Verification (NIV) loan programs. As with both programs, the source of the assets and the exact income amounts are not verified or documented. Instead, the borrower merely documents and verifies the existence of the assets and duration of the employment.

No Down Payment Program - A purchase loan programs in which the buyer avoids paying any down payment. This is sometimes called a 100% LTV loan.

No Income Verification (NIV) Loan - A non-conforming loan program that requires no documentation of the borrower's income, thus allowing a borrower to bypass the income-qualifying ratios. However, the duration and current status of the borrower's employment or self-employment must be documented.

No Ratio Loan - This program is essentially a variation of the No Income Verification loan. Unlike the "stated income" program, however, the applicant indicates no income amount in the application; the lender's underwriter ignores all income qualification questions. Such programs place the greatest underwriting weight on the applicant's credit and lowered LTV.

No-Point Rate, Program - The interest rate level of a particular program at which the borrower pays no discount or origination points.

Non-conforming Loan - Conventional mortgages that are not eligible for sale to either the FNMA, GNMA or FHLMC. Nonconforming loans (which are generally more expensive) are an alternative to the highly selective and restrictive conforming loans acceptable to Freddie Mac and Fannie Mae. Unlike portfolio loan, however, nonconforming loans are still sold on the secondary market—just not to Fannie Mae and Freddie Mac.

Non-Conforming Lender - Lender offering nonconforming loan programs, which are not sold to the secondary market through Fannie Mae or Freddie Mac.

Non-Conforming Usage - Property usage that does not meet current zoning regulations but are allowed to continue. Non-conforming usage is normally allowed through grandfather clauses. However, there are still restrictions on such non- conforming usage. Note that such non-conforming usage can be codified, expanded or permanently continued only through a variance or zoning amendment.

Non-Conventional Loan - Mortgage industry term for residential loans that are guaranteed by the government. Non-conventional programs typically refer to FHA and VA loans.

Non-Disturbance Clause - A provision in a mortgage deed that requires both the borrower and lender to continue any current lease agreements in the event of a foreclosure.

Non-Judicial foreclosure - A type of foreclosure that does not involve the courts. Unlike judicial foreclosures, this process usually gives the lender the title to the subject property (deed in lieu of foreclosure) or the power to sell the property (power of sale clause).

Non-Performing Loan - Loans that have become seriously delinquent or is in default or foreclosure are labeled non-performing loans.

Non-Recourse Loan - Sometimes called a dry mortgage, the non-recourse loan does not hold the borrower personally liable for the loan obligation. Rather, the loan holds the property and the ownership entity created by the borrower--i.e., corporation, partnership, limited liability company, etc.-- directly responsible. In the case of a default, if the property and entity cannot adequately satisfy the sums due, the lender cannot pursue the borrowers personally.

Normal Wear and Tear - Physical depreciation to property that can be reasonably expected to occur through ordinary use or occupation.

Nosing Line - Construction term referring to an imaginary diagonal line running through the front edges of a series of stairway steps. See Riser and Tread entry.

Notary Public - A person legally empowered to witness and certify the validity of documents and to take affidavits and depositions. Mortgage deeds, promissory notes and other closing documents often need to be notarized. The closing agent is normally a notary public.

Note - An instrument that indicates a promise to pay a sum of money at a specified time. The official interest rate of a loan or promissory note. Buydown and GPM loans will often lower the interest rate and payments in the initial years, before gradually increasing to the official note rate.

Notice of Default - A formal announcement delivered to a party informing or reminding that individual or entity that their loan obligation is currently in default.

Notice to Quit - A formal announcement by the tenant, delivered to the property owner or manager, that the tenant intends to vacate the rental premises.

Notorious Possession - Possession of a property that may not be formally recorded but is generally acknowledged.

Novation - The process or act of replacing a contract with a new one, while still retaining the same two parties to the contract.

Null and Void - A legal term applied to contractual agreements that is no longer enforceable.

Nuncupative Will - A will created verbally by a person near death.

Obsolescence - In the residential mortgage world, this applies to properties or elements of a property that have lost their utilitarian value.

Occupancy - The use of a property as a full-time residence by the borrower—as opposed to second home, rental or investment property.

Occupancy Level - A calculation of the percentage of the property currently occupied by tenants. This measurement may be of the number of occupied units divided by the total number of leasable units. However, the most common method for commercial properties is the square footage amount currently leased by tenants divided by the total leasable area amount.

Occupancy Statement - A statement of intent to occupy a property as primary residence, that is required for owner-occupied loan programs. Most conforming loan programs are geared for owner-occupied properties; investment properties have higher rates, fees and down payment requirements.

Off-Site Improvement - Any development or construction of land surrounding or affecting the site of the subject property.

Offer to Purchase - A preliminary agreement, secured by the payment of earnest money, between a buyer and seller as an offer to purchase real estate. An offer to purchase, or binder, secures the right to purchase real estate upon agreed terms for a limited period of time. If the buyer changes his mind or is unable to purchase, the earnest money is forfeited unless the binder expressly provides that it is to be refunded.

Office of the Comptroller of the Currency (OCC) - Federal office responsible for regulating nationally chartered banks.

Office of Thrift Supervision - An office of the U.S. Treasury department, which is responsible for regulating the S&L industry.

Oil Lease - Similar to gas leases, a landowner may give another party the right to drill for oil on that landowner's property. If no oil is found, the landowner receives a flat rent. If the lessee discovers oil and begins extraction, the landowner receives royalty payments, often in addition to the flat rent. Sometimes, the oil and gas lease rights are combined.

One-and-a-Half-Story Home - See Cape Cod entry.

One-Story Home - See Ranch entry.

Open-End Mortgage - A mortgage that allows additional money (secured by the same collateral) to be advanced by the lender. Credit lines are sometimes considered open-end mortgages.

Open House - A marketing method used in the residential real estate industry that invites prospective buyers to visit the property at the same time. Open houses make efficient use of the seller's time, as well as create a more competitive atmosphere between potential buyers.

Open Listing - Also called a simple listing or general listing, non-exclusive agreement between the seller and real estate agent that requires the seller to pay commission only if the listing agent is able to bring the buyer to the seller. If the seller finds a buyer through another agent or with no help from the listing agent, the seller will NOT have to pay any commissions to the original listing agent.

Open Mortgage - A mortgage loan obligation whose term has matured but which has not been completely settled as required. The term has expired with amount overdue and subject to foreclosure.

Operating Expense Ratio - A calculation indicating how much of the gross income must be earmarked for operating expenses. This ratio is the total operating expense for a period divided by the total effective gross income for that same period.

Operating Expenses - The costs required to maintain the operations of an investment.

Operating Lease – A subleasing arrangement, by which a lessee (tenant) leases the property to a sub-lessee who actually occupies the leased premises.

Operating Leverage - A financial method in which a small increase in the gross income results in a larger percentage increase in the net operating income.

Operating Statement - A financial statement that displays the income and expenses for an investment property for a specified period.

Opinion Letter - a written analysis and judgment from an attorney pertaining to the probable tax and legal consequences of an investment or action.

Opinion of Title - A formal analysis and certification, usually provided by an attorney or title company representative, that confirms the validity of a title to a property.

OPM - Other people's money. An investment term referring to the process of making investments with the use of borrowed funds.

Option to Purchase - The right to purchase or lease a property at a certain price for a certain period of time. For example, a lease agreement with a purchase options provides the prospective buyer with a limited option to eventually purchase the property. Any financing that the buyer obtains (after a seasoning period) often will be considered a refinance, so that down payment is not always necessary.

Option Price - The cost that an optionee must pay to obtain an option. Note that this is not the price required when exercising the option.

Oral Contract - A legally binding verbal agreement.

Ordinary Income - According to the IRS, the term ordinary income applies to any income that is taxed at regular rates--as opposed to capital gain income.. Ordinary income is typically classified into active, passive and portfolio income.

Ordinary Life Estate - One of two types of conventional life estates, the ordinary version is based on the life of the tenant. When the tenant dies, his or her ownership passes to a remainder interest or reversionary interest.

Ordinary Loss - An income tax term that applies to any losses that may be deducted from ordinary income.

Organizational Fee - The compensation that a general partner receives for services relating to the creation or development of a syndicate.

Origination - The initial loan application, processing and underwriting stages of the primary mortgage market.

Origination Fee - The charge for services performed by the company handling the initial loan application and processing. See also the Finance Fee entry.

Originator - The person or company responsible for originating a loan.

Outrigger - A beam or plank parallel to the ridge board that connects an exposed fascia rafter with interior rafters. With overhanging roofs, the overhanging rafter is attached by the outrigger to non-overhanging rafters.

Outstanding Loan Balance - The dollar amount currently remaining due (normally overdue) on a loan obligation.

Over-Improvement - Any improvements that are excessive in cost or size in relation to the value of the land and its surroundings. For example, if a given area only contains homes selling for $100,000 and a home owner decides to cover his house in gold worth much more than the average market value, that home owner has essentially over-improved his property.

Overage Lease - A lease arrangement that collects additional charges from the tenant, based on a percentage of sales that a tenant generates above a specified sales base. Shopping malls will sometimes use this arrangement as an incentive for the mall director to pursue optimum traffic to the center.

Overall Capitalization Rate - A measure of an investment property's income producing strength. This calculation is the net operating income divided by the sales price or total cost of the investment.

Overall Rate of Return - Similar to the overall capitalization rate, the overall rate of return is the net operating income divided by the purchase price of the property.

Overtime Income - Compensation for time worked in excess of regular work period. Most mortgage lenders allow applicants to use the overtime income as part of their income qualification. However, overtime income is considered unstable. So the qualifying amount is the average monthly over the past two years (24 months).

Owner-Occupied - Residential properties that the borrower occupies as a primary residence. Loans for owner-occupied properties normally enjoy better terms and pricing than do properties for second homes and investment properties.

Owner's Title Insurance Policy - A type of title insurance policy that protects the property owner against both known and latent title defects. It only covers the amount paid for the property and often has exceptions for claims that could have been discovered with a physical inspection of the subject property.

P-R

P&I - Common name for the monthly or periodic principal and interest payment.

Package Mortgage - A mortgage pledge that includes both real and personal property.

Panel (Door) - The decorative pieces between the stiles and rails of a door. Panels are integral parts of the popular panel door style. For more information about the parts and types of doors, see the Door entry.

Panel Door - A traditional type of door found in most residences. Panel doors consist of stiles, rails and panels. For more information about the parts and types of doors, see the Door entry.

Panelized Housing - A type of manufactured homes, in which wall units are produced at a factory and assembled at the final site. These walls normally come complete with electrical wiring and plumbing requirements and are fitted together like puzzle pieces at the site. Unlike mobile and most modular homes, panelized housing are standard types of housing with full foundations. The panelized design allows developers to set a building in less than a week.

Parcel - A piece of property. In most cases, a parcel refers to a specific area that is recorded with one property identification number.

Partial Release - The removal of a mortgage lien from a specific portion of the total collateral amount. In large housing developments, for example, the lender of the development loan has a lien on the entire project. However, as each new home or unit is purchased, the lender releases its lien on that specific unit. The lender keeps its liens on all of the other units or parcels.

Partial Taking - A condemnation action--undertaken through the government's or utility's power of eminent domain--that takes only a portion of the entire property from the current owner.

Participation Certificates (PC) - Securities that are collateralized by multi-million dollar blocks of geographically diverse single-family loans and offered by Freddie Mac (FHLMC).

Participation Loan - A loan funded by more than one lender. This is sometimes called syndicated loans and is common with large commercial projects, wherein a bank does not want to hold full exposure.

Particleboard - A board sheet consisting of wood scraps that have been grounded, glued and molded into a panel. Inexpensive and heavy, it is popular for interior use. However, it does not resist water very well so it is not suitable for exterior use.

Partition Right - See Right of Partition entry.

Partition Wall - A non-load-bearing wall that separates rooms.

Partnership - A form of business, property or company ownership, in which two or more individuals share ownership and control of the business' activities. A partnership provides some protection for the individual against business losses; however, it does not provide the same level of protection as does a corporation.

Party Walls - Townhouses are normally built right to each other. Often, individual townhouse units share one separating wall. Such walls are considered party walls.

Pass-Through - Expenses incurred by a property owner or manager that are charged to the tenant, per the lease agreement. In Triple Net leases, for example, the tenant is assessed for the tenant's share of the property's taxes, utilities, insurance, maintenance and operating expenses.

Passive Income - Revenue or income from investments in which the individual investor does not actively or materially participate. Limited partnerships and real estate investments are considered passive. Passive income losses cannot be used against active income. Real estate losses are always considered passive income losses; but they may be deducted against active income if the individual actively participated in at least the management decisions and personal active income is less than $150,000.

Contrast this with active income and portfolio income, which are other forms of taxable ordinary income.

Passive Investor - An individual or entity who invests in a project but does not participate in the active management or operations of that investment.

Pay Stubs - Attachments to an employee's paycheck that summarize the gross earnings, deductions and net earnings for the pay period. Most pay stubs also summarize the year-to-date earnings and deductions.

Payback Method - Any calculation measurement that produces a multiplier used in real estate investment analysis.

Payment Cap - A limit on the amount that an ARM loan's monthly payment may increase or decrease during an interest rate adjustment. Although the ARM's interest rate may increase, the actual increase to the monthly payment will be limited to the maximum set by the payment cap. Unfortunately, many payment caps incur negative amortization.

Payoff Statement - The lender invoice indicating the amount required to pay off the balance of a loan or debt obligation. Mortgage loans are usually paid off in the course of a refinance or when the property securing the loan is sold.

Per Diem - Latin phrase meaning "for each day." With mortgage loans, per diem is normally used with payoff statements to indicate the daily interest rate charge.

Percentage Lease - A lease arrangement used with many commercial retail properties, in which the lessee's rent is based on the gross business revenue that the lessee generates through the leased premises. Such an arrangement would require continuous and full financial disclosure by the tenant of the tenant's business activities. This may be either a gross lease or net lease arrangement, but there is usually a minimum rent amount and a recapture clause allowing the lessor to reclaim the property if minimum sales are not met.

Percolation - The porousness of an area allowing drainage of water into the ground. This affects septic tank and wetland requirements, which may increase a homeowner's expenses.

Perfecting the Title - See Clear Title entry.

Performance Bond - A guarantee that contracted work will be completed as agreed. Contractors may be required to provide a performance bond before beginning work. If the contractor is unable to complete the work as agreed, the bond insurer will provide funds to obtain another contractor who will complete the construction.

Perimeter Space - The defined area located along the outer borders of a property.

Period (ARM) - The length of time between rate and/or payment adjustments for adjustable-rate mortgage (ARM) loans. For example, a one-year ARM adjust rates and payments every twelve months.

Periodic Cap - With most ARM loans, interest rate adjustments from one period to the next period are normally limited by the periodic cap.

Periodic Estate - A type of leasehold estate that does not describe a specific expiration date. The lease is automatically renewed each time the periodic rent is paid and received. The lessee may leave at any time; while the lessor may terminate the lease with a proper notice (one week for weekly periods; one month for monthly periods; and 3 to 6 months for a year-to-year period).

Permanent Financing - Similar to an end loan, permanent financing refers to a long-term mortgage loan that is normally used to refinance or replace a short-term construction loan.

Personal Guarantee - A guarantee provided by an individual as endorsement for a debt. In cases of default, the personal guarantee makes the debt a personal liability and allows the lender to pursue the individual for settlement of the obligation. Compare with Non-Recourse Loan entry.

Personal Loan - A type of financing that normally has no collateral. Often called signature or unsecured loans, personal loans provide the borrower with funds with no collateral requirement. Credit cards can be considered types of personal financing because they do not require collateral. Personal loans typically have higher rates and require better credit, because of the higher risks involved.

Personal Property - Any possession of value that is not real estate.

Personalty - All assets and properties that are not permanently attached to the land. See Fixture and chattel property entries.

Pest Inspection - An inspection of a property that may be infested or property that is in an area with risks of infestation. Some loan programs automatically require a pest inspection.

Physical Depreciation, Physical Deterioration - The property's decrease in value and usefulness caused by age, normal wear and tear, negligence or natural influences. Such deterioration may be curable or incurable.

Physical Life - The period of time that a structure or property remains sound and capable of fulfilling its intended use.

Piggyback Loan - There are two definitions for piggybacks. Many use it to refer to construction-permanent loans, while most lenders use it to refer to financing that closes two simultaneous loans on the same propert.

Pilaster - Column supports, often used with foundation walls.

Pipeless Furnace System - A type of gravity heating system used for smaller houses with low heating requirements. Heated air is distributed through floor registers which also have separate cooled air intake grills attached to the same register. Installation for these systems are cheap, but they do not distribute heat evenly.

PITI (Principal, Interest, Taxes, Insurance) - Acronym used to identify the projected housing payment components of mortgage loan principal and interest, (real estate) taxes and all insurance.

Plank and Beam Roof - A style of roof framing that provides a wider expanse of space beneath the roof. The ridge beam is supported at either ends by posts. Instead of rafters, sloping transverse beams connect to the side of the ridge beam on one end and to a load-bearing post--usually along the external wall--on the other end of the transverse beam. Roof planks are then attached parallel to the ridge beam and perpendicular to the transverse beam.For wider structures additional longitudinal beams, supported by posts, may be added between the ridge beam and the walls to provide additional support. With such structures, the transverse beams are often eliminated. Instead, the roof planks are attached perpendicular to the longitudinal beams.

Planned Unit Development (PUD) - A comprehensive land development plan, used primarily in the planning and construction of residential areas, that provides for shared properties or obligations. Townhouses or subdivisions in unincorporated areas may be developed as PUDs and have homeowners associations to maintain those responsibilities within the project confines, such as snow removal, road repair and greenbelt maintenance.

Planning Department - Local municipal or county authority responsible for management and overview of development within the town, city or county boundaries.

Plasterboard - See Drywall entry.

Plat - The actual drawing of one or more parcels of land, with a focus on the division, subdivision or part of the subdivided property. See also the survey entry.

Plat Act - Laws used by some states that specify the smallest parcel of land that can be subdivided and sold.

Plat Book - A public record, usually maintained by the local county government, that contains the maps of property parcels, streets and subdivisions. Sometimes called the map book, the plat book contains plat maps and is central to the Plat of Survey system.

Plat Map - The recorded survey used in the Plat of Survey system, which describes property with recorded lots, blocks and tracts--and which become part of the legal description. This also indicates public streets, lot sizes and utility easements.

Plat Method - See the Plat of Survey System entry.

Plat of Survey System - Sometimes called the Recorded Plat or Lot-Block-Tract method, this system is one of the three common methods of surveying property. This system is used in urban areas and relies on surveyors' plat maps that have been recorded with the county and placed in the plat book. Compare with Rectangular Survey System and Metes & Bounds method.

Platform Frame - Sometimes called a western frame, the platform frame is a variation of the balloon frame method of structure frame construction. It is now the most common method used for one- and two-story homes. With platform frames, only one floor is built at a time, and each floor serves as a platform for the next story. Unlike standard balloon frames, platform framing uses shorter and less expensive studs--and the platform barrier also offers somewhat better fire protection. It is also an easier method, as wall studs are normally nailed to upper and lower plates; the pre-fab frame is then raised into place and anchored to the sill.

Pledged Account Mortgage (PAM) - A mortgage plan in which the borrower deposits a portion of the down payment in an escrow account, in exchange for initially lower monthly payments. Each month, the lender withdraws money from the escrow to supplement the borrower's payment.

Plot Plan - A schematic or plat that displays the intended or current use for a parcel of land.

Plottage - A principal of value used in appraisals, wherein adjacent lots are merged to produce a land value that is higher than the sum of the values of the individual lots.

Plywood - A popular building material consisting of panels glued together in criss-cross pattern. Some may have a lumber core. Plywood is normally graded A through D, depending on quality. CDX plywood is a C-grade and D-grade board with an external glue.

Point of Beginning (POB) - A monument or marker used to establish boundaries in a metes and bounds method of surveying. The boundaries are described by beginning and ending at the point of beginning.

Point - A unit of measure for charges on loans; one point is 1 percent of the loan amount. For example, if the borrower is assessed a 2.00-point discount fee on a $150,000 loan, that borrower must pay $3,000 ($150,000 x 2.00%) as the discount fee.

Police Powers - Legal terminology referring to one of the four basic government powers, from which the government's right to regulate private property arises. Enabling legislation by state governments allow local governments (county and city) to exercise certain police powers.

Portfolio Income - Taxable ordinary income that arises from interest, capital gains , royalties, stock dividends and annuity income. Compare this with active and passive income.

Portfolio Loan - Mortgage loans that are not directed to the secondary mortgage market or are intentionally kept by the lending institution are called portfolio loans. Lenders usually tailor their portfolio loans with more lenient guidelines (in certain aspects) than conforming loans sold to Fannie Mae (FNMA) and Freddie Mac (FHLMC).

Positive Easement - A type of easement that allows a landowner to use another persons property. For example, the owner of a landlocked property can get an easement to traverse a neighbor's property to get in or out. Compare this to negative easement.

Possession - Legal term referring to the right of a property owner to occupy property. In a lease arrangement, the property owner's right becomes a constructive possession by right of title.

Post and Beam Frame - A variation of the balloon frame and platform frame, which offers wider open spans within the building. Just as with platform framing, the walls studs only extend from floor to floor, instead of going all the way to the top of the building. The larger posts are used to provide concentrated load bearing in certain areas to allow wider rooms. Beams are attached to the posts to either support the floor above or the roof.

Powder Post Beetle - A wood-damaging insect that bores small round holes into wood. For more information, see the Infestation entry.

Power of Attorney - An agency relationship by which a principal authorizes an agent or representative to act as the principal's attorney or duly authorized representative. The three common types of power of attorney relationships are the unlimited, general and specific power of attorney relationships.

Power of Sale Clause - A provision in the mortgage deed that allows the lender to sell the property upon the borrower's default on his or her obligation, without a foreclosure suit. This is common with deeds of trust or in title theory states. The lender simply delivers and records a notice of default, and then sells the property at auction. If the selling price is insufficient, the lender may further sue for a deficiency judgment. Similar to the deed in lieu of foreclosure , this is a form of non-judicial foreclosure .

Pre-Cut Housing - A type of manufactured home construction, in which the building material are delivered to the home site pre-cut and ready to assemble. The pre-cut style eliminates or reduces the need for extensive custom cutting and adjustments at the construction site. Unlike the panelized home type, the pre-cut house normally does not pre-assemble room sections at the factory.

Pre-lease - To obtain a conditional lease commitment prior completion of the improvements and issuance of proper certificates of occupancy.

Preliminary Approval, Pre-Approval - The term used to describe the preliminary "underwriting" review and acceptance of the applicant's credit, income and employment qualification.

Preliminary Cost Estimate - The initial "ballpark figure" projection of improvement costs for a planned project

Quadraplex - A residential property containing four apartment units within one structure.

Qualified Fee - See the Fee Simple Defeasible entry.

Qualifying Income - The applicant's and property income used to calculate the borrower's ability to repay a loan. Lenders apply limits and restrictions on what type of income can be used, and how they can be calculated.

Qualifying Rate - The interest rate used to calculate the borrower's monthly payment qualification. With ARM loans, which usually have low teaser rates, the interest rate used for income-qualification is usually 2.00 percentage points higher than the low start rate.

Quantity Survey Method - A method used to estimate construction, reproduction and replacement costs that compiles an itemization of the materials required to replace the current improvements with detailed estimates of the current costs for those materials and required installation and building costs. Other methods include the square foot, cubic foot, unit in place and index methods.

Queen Anne - A popular variation of the traditional Victorian style of housing. The Queen Anne is considered a late Victorian style and is identifiable by its symmetrical design and the use of a mix of materials, patterns, shapes and colors. Victorian homes are more decorative than most American housing, and its decorative details come from many architectural styles, including Gothic, Renaissance, Romanesque and Colonial American.

Quiet Enjoyment - A legal term used with titles and leases--but with different applications. In most leases, the property owner promises to provide the tenant with the right to use the property in peace and without undue disturbance. With title conveyances, see the Covenant of Quiet Enjoyment entry.

Quiet Title Suit - A suit to remove a defect, cloud or questionable claim against the title to the property.

Quitclaim Deed - A type of deed used to convey property from a grantor to a grantee. Quitclaim deeds provide little or no guarantees to the grantee; they are normally used to cure minor or technical defects in the title.

R-Value, R-Rating - A measurement of the effectiveness of an insulation material, based on the material's resistance to heat flow. Insulation with higher R-values are better able to prevent heat loss and heat gain. Typically, minimum R-Values for walls are 11, for ceilings are 9 and for floors over crawl spaces 13. However, colder climates may require R-19 for walls, R-33 for ceilings and R-22 for floors.

Radon - An invisible gas with no odor produced naturally by the decay of uranium. It enters homes through minuscule cracks. Unfortunately, improved insulation technology has caused radon to be trapped in homes. The U.S. Surgeon General announced that radon is the second-leading cause of lung cancer, after smoking. Fortunately, radon now can be quickly detected and professionally prevented.

Rafter - With most buildings, the rafter is the skeleton base of the roof. These planks are normally cut with notched ends to fit the tops of the wall plate of the highest floor. The other ends are then angled to lean against a central board called a ridge board. To provide more support, the paired rafters are connected with collar beams or created with a truss assembly.

Rail (Door) - Construction term referring to the wide horizontal strip at the top, bottom and often middle of the door face. Therail and stile essentially frame the panels of the popular panel door. For more information about the parts and types of doors, see the Door entry.

Rail (Window) - The outer parts of the window sash. The rail is not the track on which sliding windows glide. The rails are part of the sash, not the window frame. For more information about the parts and styles of windows, see the Windows entry.

Raised Ranch - See Bi-Level entry.

Rake - The part of a gable roof that hangs over the gable end.

Ranch - Sometimes called a "one-story house," this contemporary style of houses limits the structure to one level, with an optional basement. The elimination of stairs and a second level makes maintenance easier--as well as making basic living easier for senior citizens. The ranch style normally has a larger footprint than multi-story residences, so as to offer sufficient living space. This increases the required foundation, so actual construction costs will often be the same as for a two-story home.

Range - A real estate surveying term used with the rectangular survey system, ranges refer to the columns of land between range lines. Ranges are typically numbered east or west of principal meridians. Ranges are normally used in conjunction with base lines, range lines, principal meridians, township lines, townships and sections.

Range Line - A real estate surveying term used with the rectangular survey system, range lines refer to identified lines running north-to-south across the nation, from which specific parcels of property are measured. Range lines are six miles apart, which create columns called ranges. Townships are created from the intersection of range lines and township lines. Range lines are normally used in conjunction with base lines, principal meridians, township lines, townships and sections.

Rate & Term Refinance - A refinance that repays the principal balance of an existing loan, plus (optional) the closing costs, but does not provide extra cash to the borrower. The new loan normally will have a different interest rate or term than the original.

Rate Lock - A loan registration with a lender that instructs the lender to set aside a certain amount of money for the borrower, at a specified interest rate. When the rate is locked, both the lender and the borrower are committed to closing and disbursing the loan with that interest rate—within the lock period.

Rate of Return - A percentage measurement of revenue generated by an investment for an investor. This rate divides the revenue received by the amount of the initial investment and is usually provided for a specific period. For example, an investor buys a stock for $100 and receives $5 in dividends during the first year. That investment generated a preliminary rate of return of 5%.

Rate Sheet - The listing of interest rates for different loan programs, published by each lender.

Raw Land - Land that is not improved or developed.

Real Assets - Real estate or real property owned by individual or corporation.

Real Estate - The term real estate includes land and its minerals and resources, as well as any artificial improvements affixed permanently to the property.

Real Estate Agent - Any person or property who acts as a representative and marketing agent for a property owner, for the purpose of selling a real estate property.

Real Estate Attorney - A lawyer or attorney who specializes in real estate. Although not required, attorneys are highly recommended for purchase transactions. They will review the purchase contract, monitor the processing and guide the buyer through the closing.

Real Estate Broker - A real estate agent who has been certified by the state or local regulating agency to operate a brokerage office. Only brokers can receive commission from brokered real estate sales; real estate salespeople working for the broker are designated agents and receive their compensation from the broker.

Real Estate Exchange - A tax-free or tax-deferred exchange of similar properties, permitted under Section 1031 of the Internal Revenue Code. As there is no sale, no capital gains are assessed unless one of the parties receives boot--or cash consideration--in addition to the property received in the exchange. The capital gains taxes are essentially deferred until the new owner sells the property for cash or like consideration. The most common types are multiple exchanges or Starker exchanges. A REIT is a trust that invests in real estate or real estate mortgage loans. It enjoys several tax advantages over investments in a standard real estate corporation. However, REITs are required to regularly disburse 95% of their profits to their investors. See also the Equity REIT and Mortgage REIT entries.

Real Estate Mortgage Investment Conduit (REMIC) - A type of security established by the Tax Reform Act of 1986, which allowed REMICs to issue investor-grade securities backed by a pool of mortgages. Similar to mortgage-backed securities, REMICs offered multiple classes of investment options: residual interest holders were paid as underlying loans were paid off; regular interest holders were paid on a fixed or variable rate.

Real Estate Owned (REO) Properties - Lenders who have obtained properties through foreclosure or default action often label these as REO properties.

Real Estate Settlement Procedures Act (RESPA) 0 Federal law applicable for residential property closings that requires lenders to disclose all known or estimated settlement costs for new loans, as well as provide borrower with specified disclosures regarding the loan terms, features and costs. RESPA is not applicable with all-cash, installment or assumption purchases. In addition, RESPA prohibits kickbacks between lenders and service providers, limits the reserve buffer for escrow accounts, prohibit lenders from charging a fee to prepare a settlement statement and requiring lenders to provide the settlement statement at least one day prior to closing.

Real Estate Tax - Often called property tax, real estate taxes are government assessments on real estate property. With mortgage financing, the local, county or state tax assessment on real estate property is considered part of the monthly housing obligation.

Real Property - A legal concept referring to the property rights involved with ownership of real estate. Real estate includes the land and all improvements (natural or artificial) permanently attached; while property refers to the bundle of rights involved with ownership.

Realized Gain - A term in real estate exchanges referring to a gain that one party has received. However, this gain is not necessarily subject to taxes. Compare with Recognized Gain entry.

Realtor - This title is restricted to specific real estate brokers or agents who are members of the National Association of Realtors, or one of its affiliated boards. See also the Real Estate Agent entry.

Recapture - The amount of gain charged by the IRS on the sale of depreciable property taken by the excess depreciation taken over the straight line depreciation .

Recapture Clause - A provision in a contract allowing the individual or entity who grants an interest or right to take back that such interests or rights under certain conditions.

Recertification Letter - A statement from the appraiser confirming the current validity of an old appraisal report. Recertifications are often required by lenders when the appraisal report being submitted is more than three months old. The appraiser is required to review current data and confirm that the former valuation is still applicable.

Recognized Gain - A term in real estate exchanges referring to the taxable portion of any gain that one party has received in the course of the exchange. Compare with Realized Gain entry.

Reconciliation of Value - Most appraisal reports normally calculate at least two or three value estimates, using different approaches. The three most common approaches to calculating value are comparison, income and (depreciated) cost. The official appraised value, however, is based on a reconciliation of the separate valuation approaches.

Reconstruction - In the real estate development and construction arena, reconstruction is a combination of repair and replacement of existing elements. Compare with the Repair, Renovation or Alteration entries.

Recording - Filing a legal instrument in the public records of the county. The title company is normally responsible for recording the new title and mortgage deeds from each purchase or refinance closing.

Recording Fee - Charges levied by the local government or recording office, for the purpose of recording a deed, mortgage note or other legal documents.

Records Office, Recorder of Deeds - The governmental department or office responsible for maintaining or updating real estate and other records. This recorder is usually a county level office. The records office is most important for the real estate and mortgage industry, as they make all real estate and mortgage transactions official.

Recourse Loan - Unlike the non-recourse loan, this type of obligation does make the borrower personally liable for the debt, especially in cases of default.

Recreational Property - Real estate term referring to either properties developed for primarily recreational amenities or homesites offering recreational amenities. This category would include campgrounds, RV parks or homesites that offer access to fishing, boating, skiing, etc. Compare with Entertainment Property entry.

Rectangular Survey System - Sometimes called the government survey or geodetic survey system, the rectangular survey system is one of the three most common methods for surveying property. The rectangular survey method is often used in combination with either the Metes & Bounds or Plat of Survey methods. The rectangular survey describes property location as fractions of sections, which are part of townships, and provide distance measurements from principal meridians, base lines and range lines. Because of the curvature of the earth, correction lines and guide meridians are used to compensate. A typical legal description using this system includes the (1) portion of the section, (2) section number, (3) township row, (4) range column and (5) name or number of the principal merdian. section.

Recycling (Property) - Real estate term referring to the process of redeveloping an old structure or improvement to a different usage that effectively extends its useful life.

Red Herring - A proposed investment prospectus that has not been approved by applicable government regulators.

Redemption Period - With tax sales and foreclosures, homeowners often have the option to redeem their home by paying off the tax balance or foreclosure amount. To exercise this option and keep their home, borrowers must pay off any required balance during the redemption period. See also the Right of Redemption entry.

Redlining - The unethical and fraudulent practice of refusing to provide loans, insurance coverage or financial services to the residents of a particular area--without considering the qualifications of individual applicants.

Referee's Deed - A type of deed that may be used to convey title to property in a foreclosure sale.

Refinance - Loan obtained to repay an existing loan or to place an additional mortgage lien on property currently owned by the borrower. For example, if a borrower owns a $200,000 property with absolutely no mortgage liens on it, that borrower can obtain a cash-out refinance to liquidate some of the equity.

Reflective Insulation - A type of insulation that usually consists of metal foil combined in layers, with insulating air spaces in between. This is most commonly used for roofs, walls and floors above vented or unheated spaces. For more information about types of insulation, see the Insulation entry.

Regional Shopping Center - Often called malls and supermalls, regional shopping centers are the largest category of retail shopping centers. They usually contain multiple anchors and typically include about 100 or more smaller retail shops. Regional centers normally offer more than 400,000 square feet of space.

Register - A grill-covered opening or device through which cooled or heated air is projected into a room.

Regression - A principal of value used in appraisals, wherein the value of a superior property is decreased by being next to or near poorer properties. The opposite is progression.

Regulation D - The SEC regulation that describes the necessary conditions for a private placement exemption.

Regulation Z - See Truth-in-Lending Act entry.

Rehab, Rehabilitation - Improvements performed to existing structures. All or a substantial portion of the current building's basic structure will remain. Rehabs can range from simple redecoration of internal structures to major redesign.

Rehabilitation Tax Credit - A federal tax credit available to developers who rehab commercial, non-residential buildings that were constructed prior to 1939.

REIT - See the Real Estate Investment Trust entry.

Rejection Letter, Denial Letter - The formal disclosure to the applicant of the lender's denial of the loan application and the reasons for rejection.

Release Clause - The formal element in the mortgage that releases the mortgage lien after all payments to satisfy the debt obligation have been made.

Release Deed - A type of deed used by lenders to release their claims against a property that is in a deed of trust.

Release of Lien - Legal document issued by a lien holder upon satisfaction of debt to remove its lien against a property. Also called satisfaction of mortgage, this legal document must be recorded—usually at the mortgagor's cost—to officially remove the lien from the title.

Reliction - Gradual subsiding or withdrawal of water that expands a parcel of property. Reliction is not the same as accretion that adds land to a parcel of property but not necessarily space.

Relocation Clause - A provision in a lease agreement that gives the property owner or manager the right to relocate the tenant to another, comparable site.

Remainder Interest - Legal real estate term referring to third parties receiving title to fee simple defeasible estates that have ended. When a fee simple defeasible estate ends, the title passes to a reversion interest (to the original grantor or that grantor's heir) or to an identified third party.

Rendering - An illustration created by a graphic artist to provide a three-dimensional image of the proposed improvements or development.

Renegotiate - The process or attempt to legally revise the terms of a contract or agreement. Unless the agreement specifically leaves open the renegotiation of certain elements, the other party will commonly have the right to approve or decline a request to renegotiate.

Renegotiated Rate Mortgage (RRM) - See Adjustable Rate Mortgage Loan entry.

Renewal Option - A provision in a lease agreement, allowing the tenant to renew the lease agreement, within certain terms.

Renovation - In the real estate development and construction arena, renovation involves replacing current elements of the building with new materials or elements that serve the same purpose. Compare with the Repair, Alteration or Reconstruction entries.

Rent - The consideration received from a lessee (tenant), as set forth in the lease agreement, for the lease rights to a property.

Rent Control - A form of government-imposed price control on rental rates. Such regulations normally limit the amount of rent that a tenant may be charged or restrict any increases in rental rates that a property owner may impose.

Rent Loss Insurance - The insurance coverage commonly required for many revenue properties to cover the potential loss of rental income expected for periods of vacancy that may be incurred because of an accident.

Rent Roll - A financial statement listing the tenants in a subject property and identifying their unit number, lease terms and rent.

Rent Schedule - A display of the rental rates being charged for the different units or unit types in a rental property.

Rent-Up Period - The amount of time required to completely lease the available units or space in a property after construction has been completed.

Rentable Area - See Net Leasable Area entry.

Rental Concessions - Concessions made by the property owner or manager in order to induce a prospective lessee to sign a lease agreement.

Repair - Corrective work to a property that returns it to its former functional condition, without extending its useful life.

Replacement Cost Approach - Also called the cost approach, this is a method used by appraisers to estimate the value of a property, based on the cost to produce a similar property. This approach begins with the current cost of the land and the improvements, but then depreciates that estimate according to the age and condition of the subject property. The elements of the replacement approach use one of the following methods to estimate unit costs: square foot, cubic foot, unit in place, quantity survey and index. Contrast this with the reproduction cost approach.

Reproduction Cost Approach - A method used in appraising property value that seeks to duplicate the improvements as exactly as originally constructed. No depreciation adjustments for age or condition. The elements of the reproduction approach use one of the following methods to estimate unit costs: square foot, cubic foot, unit in place, quantity survey and index. Compare with replacement cost approach.

Resale Proceeds - The net profit that a person receives from the sale of a property, after paying off all liens and closing costs.

Rescission - The act of withdrawing an agreement. Federal regulations provide homeowners who are refinancing their residence to have three full business days during which they can rescind any refinance or equity mortgage loan.

Rescission, Three-day Right of - After a residential loan is approved and closed, the borrower has three business days during which time the loan may be rescinded. If the borrower does change his or her mind and rejects the loan, the borrower may still be liable for certain origination costs. The rescission period is applicable for mortgage refinances on owner-occupied residential properties. However, there are NO rescission period required for purchase transactions or refinances on investment properties.

Reserve Requirement - Funds that borrowers must have prior to closing to demonstrate that they have the ability to make monthly payments.

Mortgage lenders often require loan applicants to demonstrate that they have sufficient funds for the down payment, closing costs, prepaid expenses, escrow deposits and reserve requirements. The reserve requirement is usually two months of PITI payments for homebuyers. It does not have to be paid to the lender; the borrower just has to show that he or she has the funds.

Resident Manager - A property manager of a multi-unit residential property, who occupies one of the units in the complex.

Residential Loan - For conforming purposes, mortgage loans for 1-4 unit, purely residential properties.

Residential Property - Property that is used for residential purposes. In the mortgage lending industry, residential property are limited to one-to-four unit properties, of which all units are used for residential purposes.

Resources Conservation & Recovery Act - A 1976 federal legislation defining hazardous substances and regulating their transfer, storage and handling. A 1984 amendment expanded the EPA's regulatory role to underground storage tanks (UST).

RESPA - See Real Estate Settlement Procedures Act entry.

Restrictive Covenant - Private restrictions limiting the use of real property. Restrictive covenants are created by deed and may "run with the land," binding all subsequent purchasers of the land, or may be "personal" and binding only between the original seller and buyer.

Resyndication - Interests or shares in a partnership that have been resold to new investors.

Retail Property - Real estate providing operating space for businesses to sell goods and services directly to customers. They yypically include shopping centers, strip centers, shopping malls and standalone stores,

Retainage - Any funds that have been set aside per the construction contract until the contractor has completed contractual obligations.

Return of Capital - The return of the original investor's capital contribution, not directly taxable.

Return on Equity - The percentage expression of the amount that is returned to the investor on his or her original investment.

Revenue Sharing - The process of distributing any profit or tax benefits among the investors in a partnership.

Reverse Annuity Mortgage (RAM), Reverse Mortgage - A type of mortgage designed to use the equity value of a home as collateral for installment payments to the borrower, usually so as to supplement an elderly borrower's living expenses. With a Reverse mortgage, the homeowner actually receives payments from the lender. The loan is recouped when the borrower dies and the property is sold or inherited by someone who can make the payments. Note that the home cannot be foreclosed as long as the borrower is alive and occupying the subject property.

Reverse Leverage - Investment term referring to a situation in which the interest rate on the property's debt servicing outpaces the owner's financial benefits from the property.

Reversion, Reversion Interest - Legal real estate term referring to the transfer of a property's title back to the grantor (or grantor's heir) when a fee simple defeasible estate terminates. When such estates end, the title can pass to such a reversion interest or to a third party remainder interest.

Revocable Trust - A type of living trust in which the original owner can be both the trustor and beneficiary and can retain the control and benefits of the trust property.

Revolving Debt, Loan - Liabilities, such as major credit cards, that do not require immediate full payment of billings or have pre- established debt and payment balances.

Rider - An addition to a contract, deed, note or covenant that amends or clarifies the original terms indicated on the document.

Ridge Board - A beam that forms the uppermost spine of the roof. Rafters are attached to the ridge board, while the other end is usually notched to fit to the uppermost external walls.

Right of First Refusal - Elements of lease, cooperative and condominium agreements that offer the holder the right to purchase or possess the subject property. With leases, the right of first refusal would allow the tenant to get the first chance to buy the property or lease additional space if the landlord seeks to sell or lease the property. With condominiums and cooperatives, the association or co-op may have the right to buy the property before the seller officially puts it on the market.

Right of Partition - A remedy available to co-owners in a joint tenancy or tenancy in common, allowing any co-owner to sue for dissolution of the co-ownership arrangement and distribution of the assets.

Right of Redemption - The right of a distressed borrower to recover property that has been transferred from their ownership, usually during a foreclosure process. To exercise this right, the borrower will have to pay off the debt obligation. Most property owners will have both an equitable right of redemption before the tax sale or foreclosure auction and a statutory right after the sale.

Right of Survivorship - Legal real estate term referring to the right of surviving co-owners to receive the ownership interest in the subject property of the co-owner who dies--instead of to the deceased's heirs. For more information, see the Joint Tenancy entry.

Right of Way - Often called an easement, the right of way is a privilege to pass through the property of another owner.

Riparian Rights - Legal concept concerning water rights for property owners whose land abuts a brook, stream, river or other flowing bodies of water. The extent of ownership depends on the navigability of the water. With navigable rivers and canals, property ownership only extends to the high-water mark at the water's edge. With non-navigable bodies of water, property ownership extends to the middle of the water stream.

Riser (Stair) - Construction term referring to the vertical height of a stairway step from tread to tread. Both the riser and tread are supported by the stringer.

Risk - The possibility that an investment will fail to produce a positive return.

Risk Return Relationship - Financial investment concept that posits high returns come primarily from high risk investments, and vice versa.

Rod - A measurement of distance equal to about 16.5 feet or 5.5 yards.

Rollover Mortgage - A mortgage loan program that structures periodic adjustments to its interest rate.

Rollover Option - A provision sometimes included in purchase options that allow the potential buyer to renew the option for a specified period, after paying specified amount.

Roof - The external top cover of a structure. There are many types of roofs now used in construction. The most common residential styles are the flat, gable, gambrel, hipped and mansard roofs. In addition, the frame used to support the roof affects the availability of usable space underneath the roof. Typical roof framing styles are conventional, plank-and-beam, sloped joist and truss frames.

Rough Plumbing - A term used to describe the installation of pipes and drains through walls, usually during the building process. Roughed-in plumbing is followed by finish plumbing, during which a plumber connects fixtures to the pipes and drains.

Routine Maintenance - Regularly and frequently occurring maintenance, such as painting, cleaning and minor repairs. Compare with preventive and corrective maintenance.

Royalty Payments - With oil or gas leases, the landowner receives royalty payments from drillers who have either oil leases or gas leases. The royalty payments are normally based on the amount of oil or gas extracted.

Run (Stair) - Construction term referring to the horizontal length of a stairway. Compare with Riser and Tread entries.

Rural - A label applied to locations outside of metropolitan (urban and suburban) areas. Such areas usually have few developments and are often primarily agricultural, wilderness or non-developed public land.

Rural Housing Service (RHS) Loan - RHS loans are the offshoot of the former FmHA programs, which sought to help housing in agricultural and rural areas of the country.

S

Sale Leaseback - A real estate investment arrangement in which the current owner simultaneously sells a property but then leases it back from the buyer. This guarantees the new owner with a rental stream, making it a more attractive investment for the buyer; for the seller, leasing the property offers liquidity and several operating tax advantages.

Sales Contract - An agreement by which property rights are transferred from one party to another.

Salvage Value - In the real estate market, a property's salvage value is its final sale value, once it has exhausted its useful life. For example, the salvage value for a residence that has completely burned down is probably only the land on which the embers smolder.

Sandwich Lease - In a subletting situation, the original lease between the lessor (landlord) and the initial lessee (tenant) is sometimes called a sandwich lease. Legally, that lease is held by the initial tenant. Thus, that tenant's lease rights are sandwiched between the lease rights of the subtenant and the ownership rights of the landlord.

Sash - Construction term referring to the part of the window that actually

117

contains the glass panes. Sashes can be either movable or fixed. For more information about the parts and styles of windows, see the Windows entry.

Satisfaction of Mortgage - The verification instrument issued by the lender to indicate that the mortgage debt has been fully paid. In contrast, a deed of trust uses a release deed. This legal document must be recorded— usually at the mortgagor's cost—to officially remove the lien from the title.

Save Harmless - Similar to a hold harmless provision, to save harmless is a legal term referring to the process of indemnifying another person. In this way, the party issuing the save harmless guarantee assumes all obligations for liabilities that may arise from a specific issue.

Savings and Loan Association (S&L) - A banking institution that solicits deposits from member customers and then lends (primarily real estate funds) to both its members and the wider community.

SBA Loan - A loan guaranteed by the Small Business Administration. These are business loans that are designed to assist small businesses with their capital, mortgage, expansion or start-up needs.

Scavenger - Trash-collection service.

Scheduled Gross Income - The projected total rental revenue expected if all rental units in a property were occupied by tenants. This figure does not take into account possible rent concessions and vacancy factors.

Schematic Design - A structural diagram of the proposed project, which takes into account all client requirements, regulatory standards, zoning and the proposed construction budget and program.

Screen Door - A type of door found in many residential properties that acts to keep out insects while providing additional ventilation to the house. Screen doors are normally placed on the outside of the regular exterior doors. Unless the homeowner has a combination door, screen doors are normally replaced by storm doors during inclement seasons. For more information about the parts and types of doors, see the Door entry.

Seasoning Requirement-Funds - Conforming guidelines demand that any funds used to satisfy down payment, closing cost and reserve requirements must come from the borrower's own resources. On a practical level, funds must be "seasoned" in the applicant's possession for at least two to three months. This typically entails two to three months of bank statements or other documentation demonstrating that funds have been in the applicant's possession. Note, however, that recent wages and salaries are often acceptable as sources for unseasoned funds.

Seasoning Requirement-Mortgage - With conforming loans, rate-and-term (No cash-out) refinances have instated seasoning guidelines on the second and other junior mortgages. If the refinance will be paying off a second mortgage with a rate-and-term refinance, that second mortgage must be at least 12 months old. Otherwise, the borrower must use a cash-out loan. What is the difference? Rate-and-term refinances allow LTVs in excess of 90%, while cash-out refinances are normally limited to 75% LTV (80% for certain homes).

Seasoning Requirement-Property - All conforming loan programs and most non-conforming programs have set seasoning requirements on the appraised property value when refinancing. Remember that the loan is limited by the LTV, which with a refinance is normally calculated against the appraised value. For example, an 80% LTV refinance on a property appraised at $100,000 is an $80,000 loan amount. However, in the first twelve months after a purchase, the LTV must be calculated against the lower of the purchase price or the appraised value. Thus, if the borrower has purchased the property for half of its true market value, that equity is essentially unattainable (with conforming loans) during the first twelve months.

Second Home, Secondary Residence - A residence, such as a summer cabin,

119

ski condominium or weekend house, that is suitable for year-round occupancy but is only occupied by the borrower for a portion of the year.

Secondary Financing - In the mortgage market, secondary financing applies to any junior mortgage loans.

Secondary Market - The market in which agencies (such as Fannie Mae or Freddie Mac) or large institutional investors purchase or sell existing loans. Agencies often resell these loans in huge blocks as mortgage-backed securities, thus replenishing the supply of funds available to lenders and borrowers.

Second Mortgage - The more common term for junior mortgage loans, which are recorded behind the first mortgage lien.

Section - A real estate surveying term used with the rectangular survey system, sections refer to the one (1) square mile (640-acre) divisions of property within a township. Each township contains 36 sections, with section #16 reserved for school usage. Sections are normally used in conjunction with base lines, range lines, principal meridians, township lines and townships. With most survey descriptions, parcels are typically described as fractions within a section. The 36 sections of each township are numbered with #1 beginning at the northeast corner, proceeding westward to #6 at the northwest section; however, section #7 is immediately south of #6 and the numbering continues eastward with #12 immediately below #1. Section #31 is at the southwest corner, and section #36 is at the southeast corner.

Section 1031 Exchange - See Real Estate Exchange entry.

Secured Credit Card - A type of credit card that requires the borrower to maintain a security deposit account with the creditor. The account is the collateral for the credit provided. These credit cards are primarily for consumers with no credit or damaged credit, who are unable to obtain standard (unsecured) credit cards.

Secured Debt - Any liability or obligation that is secured by some type of collateral. Compare this with unsecured debts.

Securities - A common term for shares or stocks in a business. This term usually refers to the ownership of those stocks or shares, which in turn represent ownership interests in the company or collateral issuing those securities.

Securities and Exchange Commission (SEC) - The government agency responsible for regulating the securities market. Because of the mortgage market's interconnection with the financial and securities markets, the SEC also oversees much of the secondary mortgage market. You may also wish to check out the SEC's website at http://www.sec.gov/.

Securitize - Mortgage industry jargon for the process of converting loans into uniform publicly traded financial securities. This is essentially what agencies such as Fannie Mae and Freddie Mac do to make more funds available for the home buyer market. See also the mortgage-backed securities entry.

Security - The collateral deposited or pledged to secure the payment of a debt. With mortgage loans, the security would be the property being mortgaged.

Security Deposit - A typical consideration item for most rental and lease agreements. With most lease agreements, the tenant is required to submit a security deposit with the landlord to cover any damage beyond normal wear and tear that may occur to the property.

Security Instrument - A legal document used to identify the collateral or security for a debt. A mortgage deed is the most obvious security instrument in the real estate market.

Security Interest - Any interest in a collateral property. For example, mortgage lenders maintain a security interest in the subject property while the loan remains unpaid.

Seed Money - Funds required to initiate any investment.

Seisin - A legal real estate term referring to the contractual description of the type of ownership interest being conveyed and the assurance that the seller or grantor has the legal authority to convey the title to a property. It is a common element in general warranty and limited warranty deeds.

Self-Amortizing Mortgage - Any mortgage loan whose regular P&I payments will eventually pay off its original principal balance by the end of the term. Most non-balloon residential loans are self-amortizing: at the end of the term--when all scheduled payments have been made--the loan is completely paid off. By contrast, at the end of the typical balloon term, a large principal balance still remains.

Self-Employment - Any form of employment, where the person works for one's self or for a company owned by that same person. Also, a 25% or more ownership of any business is often considered by most lenders to be self-employment.

Seller-Held Loan - A mortgage loan, usually subordinate to a primary loan, that the borrower-buyer owes to the property seller. The seller-held loan is sometimes used to help a marginal borrower qualify for a purchase mortgage loan. For example, it is feasible for a buyer to purchase a home with an 80% LTV conforming first mortgage loan, along with a 10% LTV second mortgage owed to the seller—the remaining 10% would then be the down payment. This is another form of creative financing.

Seller Subsidy - With purchase transactions, the seller will sometimes pay the buyer's closing costs. This is normally referred to as seller subsidy.

Seller's Market - Current economic condition in which demand is typically higher than supply. Marketing time tend to be brief, and sellers are finding an abundance of potential buyers.

Sensitivity Analysis - A systematic review of effects of different variables and assumptions on projected cash flow, revenues, expenses and profits. For example, a sensitivity analysis would examine the effect of different dramatically increased utility prices, lower occupancy rates and higher bad debt allocations on the investment property's financial statement.

Separation Maintenance - Income provided from one spouse to another, during a period of legal separation. Income from alimony, child support and separate maintenance are acceptable qualifying income for mortgage loans. However, applicants must show that (1) they have been receiving that income and (2) that income will continue for at least three more years.

Septic Tank - A common method for sewage disposal in locations without sewer access. The tank allows sewage to settle, which converts part of content into gas and sludge, while the remainder leeches into the ground.

Service Fee - In the mortgage industry, lender origination fees are sometimes called service fees.

Service Entrance - Electrical term referring to the point in the house or building at which electrical power is brought in from the electric company.

Service Panel - The main distribution point for all electrical power brought into a house or a large zone in a commercial property. Homes typically have one of two types of service panels: a fuse panel or a circuit-breaker panel. Individual fuses and circuit breakers are rated according to the amperes they can carry, which should match the capacity of the wires in the circuit. When electric flow exceeds that amp level, the fuse will melt or the circuit breaker will trip. If the wiring capacity is lower than the fuse or circuit-breaker, too much electricity could be forced through those wires, causing damage to the circuit or the fixtures.

Servicer - Any lender or related institution responsible for servicing a mortgage loan, which normally entails collection of monthly payments.

Servicing - The management of an existing loan agreement. This usually includes collecting mortgage payments, securing escrow funds and disbursing all necessary funds. Note that although conforming loans may be sold to Fannie Mae or Freddie Mac, the servicing of those loans remain with the originating lender. However, that originating lender may and often do sell those servicing rights to other lenders. Such transfers are common and legal, and the applicant will receive several disclosure of this fact and its probability.

Servicing Rights - The right to collect payments on a loan. Servicing a loan is a separate position than being the lender. The company with the servicing rights collects the payment and takes a servicing fee from the payment--but the rest of the collected funds are forwarded to the current lender or investor.

Servient Tenement - With an appurtenant easement, the property over which the easement will run. For example, lot A is landlocked and has an easement right through lot B; lot A has a dominant tenement, while lot B has a servient tenement.

Setbacks - Zoning requirements that require property construction and improvements to maintain open space from its outer boundaries. Cities regularly have setback regulations that provide for pedestrian throughway, easements and aesthetics.

Settlement - See Closing entry.

Settlement Agent - See Closing Agent entry.

Settlement Cost - The expenses normally faced by either the buyer or seller in the process of closing a purchase or refinance. Settlement costs normally include the prepaid expenses and one-time closing costs.

Settlement Fee - Cost to cover the closing services provided by the closing agent and title company. The settlement fee is separate from the closing costs, as the settlement fee is only assessed by the party responsible for the closing.

Settlement Procedures - The steps taken to finalize the funding of a loan agreement and completion of the property transfer. The settlement or closing normally requires review and acknowledgment of dozens of disclosures and legal documents—all of which are notarized and legally recorded by the closing agent.

Settlement Statement - Often called a HUD-1 Settlement Statement, this form is used for all residential transactions to provide a uniform method for recording the specific settlement entries. It was developed by the Department of Housing and Urban Development (HUD).

Severalty - A form of property ownership that is essentially the same as sole or individual ownership of property.

Severance - Real estate terminology referring to the act of converting real estate property into personal property. For example, by digging up a decorative fountain, that real property is converted into personal property. The opposite of severance is attachment.

SFR - Single-family residence, such as a single condominium unit, townhouse unit or home with no additional apartments.

Shakes - A thicker, rougher type of shingle exterior covering.

Shared Appreciation Mortgage (SAM) - A mortgage repayment plan in which the lender offers a reduced interest rate in exchange for a share of any property appreciation.

Shared Equity Mortgage - A mortgage repayment plan in which the lender holds a claim or lien on a portion of the equity that the property will accrue through appreciation. This shared equity lien is separate from the standard mortgage lien.

Sheathing - The exterior base of the house, upon which the outer walls or sidings are attached. This is usually made of wood, although additional materials are now often used to increase effectiveness.

Shed Roof - Similar to a flat roof, but with a steeper incline.

Sheet Insulation - A type of insulation in the form of a rigid board or mold. It is most commonly used as wall sheathing for cavity fill, rigid roof insulation and perimeter slab insulation. For more information about types of insulation, see the Insulation entry.

Sheetrock - A trademark name for a brand of drywall boards.

Sheriff Sale - The court-ordered auction of property to satisfy judgments against the property. When a property is foreclosed because of tax delinquency or legal judgment, for example, the court will order an auction of the property to pay off the judgment amount.

Sheriff's Deed - A type of deed used to convey to a purchaser the title to property sold by the court, usually to satisfy a judgment.

Shim - A thin, tapered strip of wood used for leveling or tightening stairs or other building elements.

Shingle - A form of exterior roof and wall covering used in many residences. Shingles are normally thin, oblong strips of covering material-- usually wood, slate or asphalt--in irregular widths. The shingles are arranged in overlapping rows to provide weather protection and decorative flourish to homes.

Shoe Trim - Construction term referring to thin decorative strips of trim placed against the bottom of base molding. For more information about the different types of trim or molding, see the Trim entry.

Shop Drawing - Construction diagrams and sketches provided by contractors and subcontractors about elements required by construction plans and agreements.

Shopping Center - A cohesive group of normally separate retail shops, stores and merchants.

Shopping Mall - A type of shopping center that provides continuous internal connections or walkways between the different merchants, shops and stores.

Short-Term Capital Gain - For income tax purposes, any capital gains that were sold before satisfying the time requirement for long-term capital gain classification.

Short-Term Loan - In the residential mortgage industry, it is any loan that matures in 20 years or less. Thus, 10-year fixed-rate loans and most balloon loans are considered short-term.

Sign Restriction Clause - The provision in most lease agreements that control, limit or prohibit the signage that the tenant may wish to post on the property.

Signature Loan - An informal term for an unsecured loan. The only collateral or guarantee for such loans is the borrower's signature.

Sill - Window construction term referring to the bottom of the window frame, into which the window is actually installed. With the head jamb and side jambs, the sill forms the window frame. For more information about the parts and styles of windows, see the Windows entry.

Sill Plate - Double boards--usually sized 2x8--laid flat and bolted to the top of the foundation walls. The building's frame is built atop the sill plate.

Simple Interest - Non-amortized calculation of the interest charge on a loan. Simple interest is solely computed against the principle balance.

Simple Listing - See Open Listing entry.

Single-Family Mortgage - A mortgage on property that may be legally occupied by only one family.

Sinking Fund - An account established by an investor for the purpose of appreciating--through compound interest--a target level at a future date. A college fund is considered by some a sinking fund: a large amount is initially deposited into the account when the child is young. By the time the child is ready to start college, compound interest should have increased that account to higher levels so as to help pay for the child's college education.

Site - A term with several usage meanings, but which essentially refers to a plot of land.

Site Plan - This variation of the standard plat displays the building lines of a subject property. It should also display the parcel's boundaries, as well as any encroachments and easement to or from the subject property.

Situs - Real estate terminology referring to people's preference for certain areas.

Skylight - A type of window that is normally attached to a roof and allows light and heat into the room. Skylights can provide five times as much heat as a standard window of the same size. Unfortunately, skylights can bring in too much heat in warmer climates while letting too much heat escape in colder climates--unless proper insulation or ventilation is attached. For more information about the parts and styles of windows, see the Windows entry.

Slab - The flat, horizontal section of a foundation, on which a structure is built. The slab, usually at least 4" thick, is placed directly on the earth or on a gravel base. In southern U.S., exposed slab foundations that are basically concrete decks are used with many ranch, mobile, modular and single-story homes. The slab itself becomes the subfloor.

Sleeper - Strip of wood placed over a concrete floor to which finished wood is attached.

Sliding Door - A type of door in which the panels slide on tracks, much like sliding windows. Sliding glass doors are common features of many homes as a doorway between the patio and family room areas. For more information about the parts and types of doors, see the Door entry.

Sloped Joist Roof - A type of roof framing, in which the ridge board is supported by a central load-bearing wall. Instead of rafters, sloped joists are connected to the ridge board on one end and the load-bearing--usually external--wall on the other end of the joist. This style, like the plank-and-beam frame allows for a more open expanse beneath the roof.

Slum - Catch-phrase description applied to urban areas and specific properties suffering from severe neglect, deterioration and deferred maintenance.

Slumlord - Derogatory term applied to real estate investors of deteriorating properties or investors who fail to make necessary reinvestments into the property required to forestall deterioration and obsolescence.

Social Obsolescence - A decrease in a property's current value that is caused by social changes and conditions that may be affecting the property and its area. For example, a well-maintained property may still lose value if its neighborhood experiences severe deterioration and neglect.

Soffit - The visible underside of structural elements such as staircases, cornices, beams, overhangs and eaves. Many homeowners and builders use aluminum and vinyl soffits to protect the roof overhangs from moisture and decay.

Soft Dollars - Expended funds that do not serve to improve the investor's equity position. For example, if the investor uses and pays commission to a buyer's broker, that commission may be considered soft dollar. Paying that commission will not improve the investor's equity position in the property just purchased.

Solar Collector - The primary device used by active solar heating system to harness the sun's rays. Water or air is forced through the collector's series of pipes. The heated air or water is then stored in a heavily insulated tank until needed.

Sole Plate - The horizontal beam or plank, upon which studs are attached.

Sole Proprietorship - A form of business ownership in which there is only one owner. For tax and legal purposes, the sole proprietor form of ownership also transfers all legal liabilities and tax benefits to the owner. For more information, compare with Partnership and Corporation entries.

Source of funds - A funding analysis that investigates the true origin of the funds that the buyer or borrower is using. For example, conforming residential lenders require full documentation of the source of funds, including two months of bank statements and explanations for any large deposits. Underwriters perform this review to ensure that the borrower's funds are legitimate and do not come from unallowed sources--such as hidden loans, which increase the borrower's debt load.

Space Analysis - A study of interior space needs to determine space requirements and plan layout.

Space Heating Systems - A localized form of heating that provides heat for a specific area or room, as compared to a central heating system. Typical space heaters include circulatory, unit, floor and resistance heaters.

Space Planning - The process of creating and implementing a layout design that best fulfills an occupant's production needs.

Spanish Colonial - A traditional style of housing that is sometimes called Mexican or Southwestern Hacienda style. The basic style usually features red tile roof, consisting of semi-spherical overlapping tiles. The wall is traditionally adobe, but is now often stucco or painted concrete block. This style also often contains oval top windows and doors, as well as wrought-iron decorations.

Special Agent - A representative in an agency relationship who is authorized to act on behalf of the principal in a specific

transaction.

Special Assessment - An additional real estate tax assessed toward a portion of the entire taxable community by a local tax authority for a special project. Special assessments are normally used to cover specific improvements, such as street improvements, commercial development or the creation of special amenities (such as zoos and museums) that is meant to benefit only a portion of the community.

Special Lien - Any lien that is applied to only specific parcels or types of properties.

Special Purpose Building - Any structure or improvement that is designed primarily or solely for the operating needs of its occupant. For example, stand-alone restaurants, movie theaters, gymnasiums and parking garages are normally considered special purpose buildings.

Special Warranty Deed - Sometimes called a limited warranty deed, this deed does not provide the grantee with the same guarantees as a general warranty deed. The special warranty deed usually only provides a covenant of seisin and a covenant against encumbrances limited to encumbrances occurring after the grantor originally acquired the title. This type of deed is commonly used by agents of the owner, such as executors.

Specific Lien - A claim against a specific property, rather than all of a person's properties. Real estate taxes and mortgage loans, for example, are typically specific liens. Compare with general liens.

Specific Performance - Legal term referring to an action required by an agreement or any action that initiates the performance of a contract.

Specific Power of Attorney - A type of power of attorney relationship in which the attorney or agent is charged with and authorized to act on behalf of the principal for a specific transaction, contract or event.

Specifications - Detailed instructions regarding the manner, material, design and schedule of work to be done by the contractor or subcontractors.

Specified Funds - Any funds whose list of target properties to be purchased has already been defined.

Speculation - Investment tactic that seeks to resell properties for a quick profit. Speculators tend to prefer holding properties for short-term periods and target areas that show potential for rapid value appreciation.

Speculative Building - Real estate investment practice of starting construction or development, without any lease or purchase commitments.

Split Entry - See Bi-Level entry.

Split-Level - Contemporary style of residential housing that offers a versatile use of space and design. The typical split level looks much like a two-story, but actually has three or four separate levels. The key element of the split level is that it contains at least one level that is a half-flight difference from the adjoining levels. For example, the bottom level may be a below-grade basement; a half-flight above the basement (but the side not above it) is the extra level, which may be the garage or a family room; directly above the basement and a half-flight up and beside that split-level space is additional living space; a fourth floor, in the split level area, may be used for bedrooms.

Spot Survey - A type of survey that indicates the location of improvements, along with the lot lines. A quick review can then reveal any encroachments.

Square Foot Method - The most common method used to estimate construction, reproduction and replacement costs uses the square footage costs of similar properties and multiplies that rate by the area of the subject property. Other methodsinclude the cubic foot, unit in place, quantity survey and index methods.

Square Footage Price - A method for comparative pricing that bases the property's total cost on its size. This is the standard method used for commercial properties.

Squatters Rights - A legal right, with varying conditions, in many jurisdictions that allow individuals to obtain a legal easement to a property. If a squatter is permitted to occupy for the proscribed statutory period a real estate property to which he or she has no legal claim, that squatter can file for and receive an easement for that parcel of property. Squatters often must be forcibly evicted with court order and supervision to protect the current owner's full ownership.

Stack Pipe - A vertical pipe that receives drain and waste lines from fixtures and delivers them to the building drain. The upper portion of the stack pipe often protrudes through the roof to vent waste gasses.

Stack Vent - Pipes attached to the stack pipe--as well as the stack pipe itself--that vents waste gases, while brining in outside air pressure to push water down the drain pipes.

Standard Parallel Line - See Correction Line entry.

Standby Fee - The charge that a lender assesses a borrower for a standby loan commitment.

Standby Loan - A loan approved for a client, but not yet closed and disbursed. The formal closing of the standby loan is normally conditional on specific events or actions. The standby loan is often nothing more than a loan commitment.

Standard Tenant Improvement Allowance - The amount that a landlord will expend in making improvements for a tenant. This allowance is not charged to the tenant. Rather, it is what the landlord or property manager believes is economically feasible to absorb.

Starker Exchange - A type of tax-deferred real estate exchange with a delayed term. This option gives the seller more time to find a like-kind property. For a Starker exchange, the proceeds from the sale of a property must go into an trust company escrow that the seller must not control. The seller then has 45 days to find and 180 days to purchase a like-kind property, which is then bought with the escrowed funds.

Start Rate - The beginning interest rate of a mortgage loan. With ARM loans, it is the interest rate for the first period, as the ARM rate will adjust in subsequent periods. With 2-1 buydown loan, for example, the starting rate is two (2) percentage points lower than the note rate. The start rate is usually lower than current market rates, in order to help the applicant qualify for a larger loan amount.

Stated Income Loan - This program is essentially a variation of the No Income Verification loan. With the stated income loan, the applicant merely states an income, and the lender will accept (or ignore) it as the qualification income. Such programs place the greatest underwriting weight on the applicant's credit and lowered LTV. Also see the No Income Verification and No Documentation Loan entries.

Statuary Lien - Any lien created by law.

Statute of Frauds - The state laws that require real estate agreements to be in writing in order to be enforceable in law.

Statutory Right of Redemption - Many states have laws that give a borrower a limited period after both tax sale and judicial foreclosure to pay off the debt and reclaim the mortgage property. This period is often called the statutory redemption period. Prior to the foreclosure sale of the home, the property owner can exercise his or her equitable right of redemption.

Steam - Water boiled to 212 degrees Fahrenheit, the temperature at which water turns to steam--but does not yet evaporate.

Steam Heating System - A type of gravity heating system that distributes heat to radiators with steam, instead of hot water. It is a noisy, but efficient system for smaller buildings that are not continuously occupied.

Steering - The unethical and fraudulent real estate practice of directing prospective homebuyers and renters away from particular areas, so as to maintain that area's homogeneity. This is considered an illegal attempt to promote segregation.

Stepped-Up Basis - A change in the adjusted tax basis that a property may use with certain transactions.

Stick-Built - Any structural improvement that uses a wooden frame. These are normally limited to low-rise residential and small commercial buildings, as they do not offer the structural strength of steel and similar metal frames.

Stigmatized Property - Properties that have become less attractive or marketable by being the scene of a crime, suicide, undesirable event or any non-physical defect.

Stile (Door) - Construction term referring to the solid, wide vertical strips normally found on the sides of the door face, as well as sometimes down the center of the door face. The stile and rail frame the panels on the

135

popular panel door style. For more information about the parts and types of doors, see the Door entry.

Stipulations - The terms, provisions, conditions, assumptions and clauses of an agreement.

Stop Molding - A type of trim-work placed between the door casing and the door or between the window casing and the window sash.

Stop Clause - A provision in some lease agreements that place a limit on the amount of operating expenses that a property owner or manager must absorb. Any amounts above that level become the tenant's obligation.

Storm Door - A type of door used in many homes to protect the regular exterior door during winter and rainy seasons, as well as to reduce heat loss through the prime door during the winter. Storm doors are usually made of aluminum or light metal frame and placed outside of the exterior door. For more information about the parts and types of doors, see the Door entry.

Straight Lease - See Gross Lease entry.

Straight Line Depreciation - The method of depreciation permitted by the IRS. The annual depreciation is a constant equal to the total depreciable basis divided by its depreciable life, as determined by the IRS published tables.

Strata Title Act - See Condominium Act entry.

Straw Man - Informal name for a person or entity who purchases property for another person or entity. The straw man buys the property from the seller and then immediately resells the property to real buyer. The straw man tactic is often used to keep the real buyer's identity private, although it can also be used to arrange a two-part sale in a no down payment program.

Strict foreclosure - A type of judicial foreclosure , in which the court does not sell the property. Instead, the court gives title to the lender and ends the debt. However, this process also eliminates all redemption rights, deficiency judgments and any surplus compensation to the borrower. This is not commonly used.

Stringer - Construction term referring to the diagonal stairway frame, which is cut to receive risers and treads.

Strip Center - Usually a smaller version of the neighborhood shopping center, the strip center format arranges the retail units in a line of relatively narrower buildings. It is often called a strip mall.

Structure - Informal term for any constructed improvements to land. It can be anything from a small shed or cabin to an apartment building or skyscraper.

Stucco - A type of textured wall covering that has proven to be a durable exterior siding for homes and buildings. It is usually applied in three coats, with the finish paint included in the final covering. Stucco is a concrete and lime mixture that creates a light pebbled look to the wall. It is sometimes difficult to apply and can crack if applied incorrectly.

Stud - Vertical wall framing members, traditionally made of 2x4 lengths of wood.

Subchapter-S Corporation - Often called an S-corp, this form of business entity is a combination of the general corporation and a partnership. Stockholders enjoy the limited liability of a limited partnership but avoid the double taxation of a corporation. However, S-corps are limited to 75 or fewer shareholders.

Subcontractor - The provider of specialized construction or improvement services. The subs usually answer to a general contractor, who supervises and directs the entire project. Typical subcontractors include plumbers, drywallers, masons and painters.

Subdivision - The act of legally separating a parcel of property from the other parcels or larger division in a defined community. A developer, for example, may purchase a farm that was legally considered one big parcel and subdivide it into smaller parcels. Subdividing requires local approval and several legal filings. The name "subdivision" is also often applied to the finished product of the subdividing process.

Subflooring - An under-layment or base for the finish flooring material. This usually consists of plywood panels attached to the floor joists. The subflooring also acts to stabilize the joists.

Subject to Condition Precedent - A legal real estate term applying to fee simple defeasible estates, this identifies the conditions that must be met for the estate to continue. Once the approved usage ceases, the estate would terminate, at which time the title would then transfer to a reversion interest or remainder interest. For example, a philanthropist grantor may give some land in a fee simple defeasible estate to a charity as long as it is used for charitable purposes. If that charity tried to do non-charity work, their estate would end.

Subject to Condition Subsequent - A legal real estate term applying to fee simple defeasible estates, this identifies the prohibited uses that would trigger the end of the estate, at which time the title would then transfer to a reversion interest or remainder interest. For example, a grantor may give his nephew his mansion with a fee simple defeasible subject to condition subsequent that he never marries; if his nephew does marry, the estate would end.

Sublease - The secondary lease in which a tenant leases out the property to another tenant. The original lease between the tenant (lessee) and the landlord remains. However, the original tenant's lease rights are now transferred to the sublessee. Most landlords wisely place limitations on subletting of their rental property.

138

Subordinate Financing, Loan - Any mortgage loan that is inferior in liens to the first mortgage. Subordinate loans are second or junior mortgages.

Subordinated Ground Lease - A ground lease format in which the owner (lessor) of the land agrees to subordinate his or her recorded interests behind other claimants. For example, a subordinated ground lease would place the lessor's claim behind any liens imposed by construction, development and mortgage loan lenders.

Subordination - To make one claim (or lien) inferior to that of another claim (or lien). Remember that liens are recorded and normally honored in chronological order. However, if a borrower refinances only the primary mortgage but not the junior mortgage on a property, the junior mortgage must be subordinated to the new refinance loan. The second mortgage lien lender must sign a subordination agreement prior to the closing, allowing the new first mortgage loan to accept primary lien.

Subordination Clause - The provision in a mortgage deed that regulates the possible subordination of the mortgage to another mortgage lien. The subordination clause of first mortgage loans prohibits its subordination to other private obligation liens. Second mortgage loans normally allow subordination, with the case-by-case approval of the lender's underwriter.

Sub-Prime Loan - Non-conforming loans that cannot be sold to the A-paper secondary mortgage market are considered sub-prime loans. Such loans are normally used for borrowers, properties or situations that cannot qualify for conforming programs.

Subrogation - Similar to a transfer of rights, subrogation is a legal term referring to the replacement of one individual or entity with another in the context of specific rights, interests or obligations. Through subrogation, insurance companies receive the policy holder's right to defend against a claim.

Subscription - A real estate legal term referring to a binding agreement to purchase an interest in a syndicated security.

Substitution Clause - In construction agreements, the substitution clause identifies those construction material that may be substituted, within the restrictions specified by the property owner, agent or developer.

Subsurface Rights - Legal real estate term referring to property rights involved with the natural subsurface elements of real estate. Subsurface rights include mineral rights, and subsurface rights can be separated from other real estate property rights. For example, a landowner may allow oil leases, gas leases or sale of mineral rights.

Suburb, Suburban - Municipalities and developed areas surrounding a city. Isolated non-developed and unincorporated areas are normally considered rural.

Suit for Rent - A legal remedy available to landlords who have lessees in default or delinquency, for the purpose of recovering past-due rent.

Sump Pump - A tool to pump water out of or through sump drainage wells.

Super Regional Center - An even bigger version of the regional shopping center, the super regional normally contains a minimum of 750,000 square feet of retail space and at least three or more anchors.

Superfund Amendment & Reauthorization Act (SARA) - A 1986 federal legislation amending the CERCLA legislation of 1980, which established the EPA's mandate with regard to hazardous or Superfund sites. SARA defined stringent clean-up standards. It also expanded the scope of liability for recovering clean-up costs, but created immunity standards for certain landowners.

Superfund Site - A property deemed to contain hazardous pollutants by the EPA and requiring clean-up. Unlike brown fields, Superfund sites normally do not allow any further activities on the site until clean-up is completed.

Supply and Demand - Economic principle describing the basically three-part relationship between the supply, demand and price of certain goods. A high-supply and low-demand market will create lower prices (deflation). A low-supply and high- demand market will create higher prices (inflation). A subsidiary concept of the law of supply and demand is that the market tends to adjust itself toward equilibrium.

Surety - A guarantee on the performance of an individual or entity. For example, a surety bond provides an insured guarantee that a service provider will perform the contracted work covered by the surety. If not, the surety company will reimburse the insured's client for losses.

Survey - The examination of land by a registered surveyor, so as to determine the property's exact geographic location and size. A new survey is required with each (purchase or refinance) loan application—although a less expensive location note endorsement from the title company is acceptable during refinances. There are three basic methods for conducting a survey: the metes and bounds method, the rectangular survey system and the plat of survey method. A spot survey will indicate the building lines, while the more detailed topographical survey provide a more three-dimensional description of the property.

Survey Sketch - A survey that illustrates the location and dimensions of a parcel of land. Compare with the Spot Survey entry.

Survivorship, Right of - An element of property title ownership that affects how assets are handled when a co-owner is deceased. When there is a right of survivorship on a property ownership, if one co-owner dies, the ownership share of that deceased co-owner is given to the surviving co-owner(s). This option applies to the ownership form normally referred to as "joint ownership with right of survivorship."

Sweat Equity - An ownership interest in property earned by the

141

performance of manual labor on that property.

Swing Loan - Short-term loan used to qualify for a mortgage loan on a new home while awaiting for a current mortgage property to be sold.

Syndicate - A legal association created to make real estate investments. The syndicate can be a partnership, joint venture or similar association.
However, syndicates are normally created for a specific investment property or project.

Syndication - A group of individuals or companies who join together to pursue a limited investment purpose. It is also the act of obtaining mortgage financing for one project from a group of institutions. Many commercial lenders will syndicate with other institutions when financing a large commercial project, so as to avoid absorbing the entire risk exposure for the loan. In the real estate industry, syndications are often limited partnerships formed to operate a real estate investment. The general managing partner is the syndicator.

T

Tacking - A promise to make a loan at a future time; this usually refers to higher-cost, shorter-term, back-up commitments used as a support for construction financing until a suitable permanent loan can be secured. Tacking may also refer to the joining of two time periods, such as when possession periods may be combined to satisfy an easement requirement.

Takeout Loan - A promise to make a loan at a future time; this usually refers to higher-cost, shorter-term, back-up commitments used as a support for construction financing until a suitable permanent loan can be secured.

Taking - A legal term referring to the government's seizing of private property through its right of eminent domain.

Tar and Gravel Roof - Often called a built-up roof, this type of covering is used primarily on flat and low-pitched roofs. It normally consists of alternating layers of roofing felt and hot tar, with a final sprinkling of fine gravel, which prevents the sun from melting the tar.

Tax Basis - The net book value of a property. To determine the tax basis value, capital improvements made are added to the original purchase price. Any depreciation taken is then subtracted from that amount. When the property is sold, the capital gains tax is calculated as the new sales price minus the tax basis.

Tax Certificate - Taxing authorities will often sell unpaid real estate taxes in the form of tax certificates. If the tax certificate is not paid within the proscribed redemption period, the buyer-owner of the tax certificate will have the right to foreclose on the property.

Tax Deductibility, Deductible - The type of expenses that can be used to reduce a person's or entity's taxable income. For example, homeowners can deduct the interest they pay on their home mortgage loan against their taxable income.

Tax Deed - A type of deed that may be used to convey title for property sold for delinquent taxes.

Tax Deferred Exchange - See Real Estate Exchange entry.

Tax Deferred Income - The act of delaying the payment of taxes on certain income until a later date. For example, certain retirement accounts allow the individual to delay income tax payments on some of the amounts deposited into such accounts. This has the effect of lowering the person's current taxable income.

Tax foreclosure -

The sale--usually through public auction--of properties that have not paid delinquent property taxes. Most local taxing authorities assure themselves of property tax revenue by selling delinquent property taxes to investors. These investors or the taxing authority can then exercise their rights to foreclose on the property. However, property owners may be able to rescue their homes by exercising their equitable or statutory rights of redemption.

Tax Increment Financing (TIF) District - A tool used by local and state governments to focus additional investment dollars for a target area. When an area is designated a TIF district, the local taxing authority will determine the tax revenue that the target area currently generates for the city, county, state and other entities. Any future tax income above that annual level that is generated from that area during the life of the TIF designation will stay in that area. That anticipated additional tax revenue can be used to improve local infrastructure, finance investments or reimburse investors. Note that tax rates are not increased, the increased revenue will come from the added business that investments will bring to that area.

Tax Map - A diagram published by most local government property taxing authorities that indicates the type and classification of those properties subject to tax assessments.

Tax Return - The form used to report income tax payment calculation. Most lenders will require copies of tax returns to document income for qualification purposes. The employee can then use this W-2 to complete his or her tax returns, as well as maintain documentation of employment and income.

Tax Sale - See the Tax foreclosure entry.

Tax Service Agency - When an escrow account is present, the tax service agency or department will assist the lender in payment of real estate taxes. When no escrow is maintained, the tax service agency or department will often monitor the borrower's payment of real estate taxes.

Tax Service Fee - The charge levied by the lender to hire a tax service agency or to compensate its own tax service department.

Tax Shelter - Investments or maneuvers that can produce opportunities to lower income or capital gains taxes. Changes to the tax codes have severely hampered most tax shelters. Previously, paper losses from real estate investments could be used to offset taxable personal income. No longer. The IRS now distinguishes between passive and active income: losses from passive income such as most real estate investments can only be offset against other passive income. Passive income losses cannot be offset against active income.

Taxable Income - The amount of a person's or entity's income that may be taxed by the IRS. This calculation of taxable income begins with the gross income, but then subtracts all allowable deductions.

Teaser Rate - The low starting interest rates offered by many ARM and Temporary Buy-down loan programs.

Tenancy at Sufferance - Legal term referring to the type of leasehold estate created when a lease has terminated or expired, but the lessee continues to occupy the leased premises. This is not considered trespassing, because the original entry was legal. If the lessor decides to accept a rent payment, this becomes a periodic estate.

Tenancy at Will - Legal term referring to a license to use or occupy a property, subject to the will of the property owner. This type of leasehold estate can be terminated by either party, with adequate notice. It is automatically terminated upon sale of property or the death or insanity of either lessor or lessee.

Tenancy by Entirety - Similar to Joint Tenancy with Rights of Survivorship, this form of ownership is only available to married couples and considers the husband and wife as one legal entity. If one dies, the surviving spouse receives full ownership of the property; the interests of the deceased does not go to any other heir unless both owners die. This form also provides an added legal protection: the property can only be sold to satisfy a judgment if both spouses signed the obligation. If, for example, only the wife signed a mortgage that went into default, the property cannot be sold--unless the husband also signed the mortgage note or a waiver of his rights. This form does not allow for a right of partition, any dissolution must be by mutual agreement or court order.

U-V

UFMIP - See Upfront Mortgage Insurance Premium entry.

Underground Storage Tanks (UST) - Tanks used to store fuel and other chemicals are now a major concern for the EPA. To prevent dangerous leakage and leeching of hazardous substances, USTs must be certified and meet strict maintenance requirements.

Underlayment - The top layer of plywood, often used above the subflooring and to which the finished floor, tiles or carpeting is attached.

Underwriter - The person or company responsible for analyzing and approving a mortgage loan application. The underwriter decides whether a loan application is worth the risk.

Underwriting - The stage of the lending process during which the elements of a loan application are analyzed so as to determine approval or rejection of file.

Underwriting Fee - A closing cost charged by mortgage lenders to underwrite a loan for approval. It is normally not charged unless the loan is approved.

Undivided Interest - Legal term referring to a type of property ownership in which two or more parties share ownership in the entire property--and not for a specific portion. The co-owners may own different percentages of the entire property.

Unencumbered Property - Any property with a free and clear title.

Uniform Partnership Act - A model act adopted by many states, which governs the types, structure, rights, requirements and limitations of partnerships. Properties held in the partnership's name are considered tenancy in partnership.

Uniform Residential Loan Application (URLA) 1003 - The standard four-page application form required for all residential mortgage loan applications, sometimes referred to as the 1003 form.

Unilateral Contract - An agreement in which one party's obligations are contingent upon a second party's performance. However, the second party has no obligation to perform and faces no penalty for non-performance.

Unimproved Property - See the Raw Land entry.

Unincorporated Area - Any parcels of land that is not part of legal municipal boundaries. These areas are governed by the county's zoning board, which are usually more lenient than municipal zoning boards.

U.S. Coast Guard & Geodetic Survey Datum - A datum used by many U.S. surveyors to measure elevations, this datum is set for the mean sea level in New York City harbor.

Unit Deed - A legal instrument used to convey the title to a condominium unit, as well as its common elements.

Unit In Place Method - A method used to estimate construction, reproduction and replacement costs that is based on the construction cost of individual building components. Other methods include the square foot, cubic foot, quantity survey and index methods.

Unit - A real estate term for apartments or each single-family portion of a property or structure.

Universal Agency - An agency relationship in which the agent represents the principal in all matters that can be legally designated to others. An unlimited power of attorney is most often used to create this type of agency.

Unleveraged Property - Any property that does not have a debt obligation or mortgage lien attached to it.

Unleveraged Program - A type of limited partnership whose real estate investments are focused primarily on properties with specific debt obligations at less than 50% of the value of each property.

Unlimited Power of Attorney - A type of power of attorney relationship in which the attorney-agent is charged with and authorized to conduct all of the principal's legal, financial and related affairs. Unlike the general and specific variations, the unlimited power of attorney allows the agent to act for the principal in all matters.

Unrealized Gain - Real estate term referring to potential profit that a property owner fails to exploit. Unrealized gain specifically occurs when the sales price is below the market value of the property. For example, a distressed or relocating property owner may be will to sell a property for less than its market value in exchange for an immediate sale.

Unsecured Loan - Loan made without any pledge of collateral or security. For example, personal (signature) loans, student loans and credit card debts are essentially unsecured liabilities, as there is nothing for the creditor to repossess in case of default.

Upfront Mortgage Insurance Premium (UFMIP) - A one-time mortgage insurance premium charged on FHA loans. This fee is usually equal to 1.75% of the loan amount and is added to the loan balance. If the borrower should eventually refinance the FHA loan with a conventional loan, this premium is refunded to the borrower on a prorated basis. In addition to this one-time upfront fee, FHA loans also assess a monthly mortgage insurance premium.

Urban - The urban label normally applies to both major cities and their suburbs. However, strictly speaking, the real estate and mortgage industry prefer to use the urban label on areas within the boundaries of major cities.

Usable Area - A property measurement used in commercial real estate, especially with rental properties. The usable area measurement subtracts unusable areas (such as bathrooms, staircases, utilities, mechanical equipment, walls, columns, easements and encumbrances) from the total square footage.

Use Clause - A provision in a lease agreement specifying the allowed usage for the leased premises.

Useful Life - An appraisal term referring to a projection of the number of years that a property will still be able to perform its intended purpose.

UST - See Underground Storage Tank entry.

Usury - In technical terms, usury is when the lender charges interest rates in excess of the caps set by state usury laws.

Utilities - The basic services and products essential to the operation of a production property. This term is normally applied to electric, gas, sewer, telephone and water services.

Utility Easement - An easement to or through a property that is established to provide utilities for the specific property or the larger community.

VA Funding Fee - A one-time charge assessed at closing to the borrower on VA loans. This fee is usually between 1.25% to 2.25% of the loan amount, depending on the down payment amount; this fee is usually rolled into the loan amount.

VA Loan - See Veterans Administration Loan entry.

Vacancy Factor - The percentage level of unoccupied units in a rental property. The vacancy factor is the inverse of the occupancy rate. It is usually expressed as a projected vacancy factor or a current vacancy rate.

Vacant Land - See Raw Land entry.

Value - The monetary worth of a property, asset, product or service. The value is normally interpreted as the amount at which the market would pay for the product at a given time.

Vapor Barrier - A sheathing material used to prevent moisture, water and vapors from penetrating into a structure. Most foundations are set on a gravel base with a waterproof vapor barrier between the foundation slab and the ground.

Variable Expenses - As opposed to fixed expenses, real estate variable expenses are those operating costs that tend to fluctuate according to the occupancy level.

Variable Lease - A type of lease arrangement that provides for future rent adjustments. There are two types of variable leases: graduated and index.

Variable Rate Mortgage (VRM) - One of the original terms for adjustable rate mortgage (ARM) loans.

Variance - An exception to zoning codes and ordinances. This does not change the zoning laws. If a property owner wishes to make improvements or changes to his or her property that do not follow local zoning requirements, that property owner must first obtain a zoning variance from the zoning authority. For example, if a developer wishes to convert a current warehouse zoned manufacturing into a residential condominium project, that developer must first obtain a variance.

Vendee's Lien - A lien placed against a property by a former buyer. If purchase transaction fails to consummate because the seller does not deliver the title, the buyer (vendee) may file a lien against the property to prohibit its sale or recover damages.

Vendor's Lien - A lien placed against a property by a seller, particularly if the full purchase price has not been received.

Verification of Deposit (VOD) - Form used by the lender to verify the contents and records of a loan applicant's accounts with a depository institution. This is required for all loan application files.

Verification of Employment (VOE) - Form used by the lender to verify the status, income and stability of applicant's employment. This is required for all loan application files.

Verification of Loan (VOL) - Form used by the lender to verify the contents and records of a loan applicant's current loan account. This is required only if the borrower has an outstanding loan that is not listed in the credit report.

Verification of Mortgage (VOM) - The form used by the lender to verify the mortgage account of an applicant. The VOM is necessary only if the mortgage account is not reflected in the credit report.

Verification of Rent (VOR) - The form used by the lender to verify the rent-payment record of first-time home buyers.

W-Z

W-2 - The official IRS-designated form that employers must use to report the employee's income for the year. Employers must provide the employee with a copy of the W-2 form submitted to the IRS. The employee can then use this W-2 to complete his or her tax returns, as well as maintain documentation of employment and income.

Waferboard - Wood panels composed of wooden flakes that have been glued together under high pressure. It tends to swell when exposed to moisture, but can still be used for roof decking and wall sheathing in select circumstances.

Wages, wage-earner - In the mortgage underwriting arena, the term wages apply to income compensation that is based on an hourly calculation. Wage-earners, as opposed to salary-earners, are paid for each hour worked and receive additional compensation for overtime.

Wainscot - A facing or paneling on the walls of a room. The term is also used to describe the lower part of a wall when it is made of a different material from the upper portion of the wall. The trim that separates the wainscot from the upper portion of the wall is the chair rail.

Walkthrough - See Final Walkthrough entry.

Wall Plate - A horizontal beam attached to the top of frame studs.

Warehousing (Loans) - The process by which a warehouse mortgage lender originates loans in the primary mortgage market, with the intention of selling those loans to the secondary mortgage market when a minimum volume is achieved. The business model of such lenders is focused on originating loans, not servicing them. Warehouse lenders usually have forward commitments with investors in the secondary market to provide those investors with qualified loans.

Warehouse - Property used for storage of inventory and personal property.

Warranty - A promise offered by one party to another in a legal agreement. See also Home Warranty entry.

Warranty Deed - A method of legally conveying property, in which the buyer receives assurances and guarantees from the seller regarding the validity of the title being transferred.

Warranty Forever, Covenant of - An element of a general warranty deed that guarantees that the grantor will compensate the grantee for any losses or expenses to defend the title being conveyed against any party claiming superior claim to the property.

Warranty of Title - See Warranty Forever entry.

Waste - A real estate term referring to damage of property, particularly by a lease tenant or life tenant.

Water Heater - The fixture that provides heated water to the hot-water system of a house or building. Water heaters are usually heated by gas, oil or electricity. Gas and oil heaters tend to be cheaper, but need ventilation. Water heaters are usually separate from the boiler system that heats some buildings, although some buildings do use the boiler as a source for hot water. The water heater typically consists of a tank that receives cold water, heats it and stores it until it needs to be delivered through the hot-water system. Most single-family homes require a 40- to 60- gallon tank.

Water Rights - Real estate term referring to ownership interest in bodies of water along a property owner's parcel, as well as the right to draw large amounts of water from such sources. Water rights normally include riparian rights, littoral rights and prior appropriation rights.

Water Softener - A mechanical system used to soften the hard water--water with more than five grains of salt (carbonates and sulfates) per gallon-- found in much of the U.S. Hard water tend to clog pipes, leave scum and complicate washing. Water softeners pass the water through a bed of resin and a silica sand filter to absorb the salts. Typical systems have a second tank of brine that regenerates the brine, which regularly loses its efficiency.

Watts - A measurement of electrical power equal to the amperage of a current times its voltage. Wattage provides a measurement of the amount of power required by a device or set of devices.

Weep Hole - Construction term referring to holes at the bottom of brick and masonry walls that allow water to escape from the space between the bricks and building sheathing.

Western Frame - See Platform Frame entry.

Wet Columns - Building columns that contain or are designed to contain pipes for plumbing fixtures.

Wholesale Lender - A lender who funds mortgage loans originated through brokers or correspondents, and then sells those loans to investors in the secondary market. Some wholesale lenders are warehousers.

Will - The legal instrument to control the disposition of a deceased individual's property and assets. A person who dies with a will has died testate; to die without one is intestate. The deceased who made the will is the testator or testatrix. The will's disposition of property is called a devise, and the receiver is the devisee. The assets transferred is a bequest.

The will is filed with probate court, and the administrator of the will is the executor or personal representative. In addition to the standard will, there are also holographic wills and nuncupative wills.

Window - Wall openings designed primarily to provide a view of the outside, as well as provide ventilation and light. Typical windows normally consist of energy efficient glass, jambs, sashes, muntins, sills and rails.

The most common styles of window designs are awning, bay, casement, double-hung, fixed, hopper, horizontal sliding, jalousie, skylight and triple-track windows.

Winged Gable - A type of gable roof with more pronounced overhangs.

Without Recourse - See Non-Recourse Loan entry.

Words of Conveyance - See Granting Clause entry.

Working Capital - Finance term referring to the current assets available to a business after subtracting all current liabilities.

Work Letter - Real estate term referring to the provision in the lease agreement that stipulates the work that the landlord, property manager or owner must perform for the tenant.

Workout Loan - A finance arrangement in which the lender has agreed to lower the borrower's payment requirements in order to prevent a foreclosure .

Wraparound Mortgage - A junior mortgage that acknowledges and includes an existing mortgage loan in its principal amount due and in its payment conditions. Payment is made to the lender of the wraparound mortgage, then that lender makes payments on the previously existing mortgage loan(s).

Writ of Attachment - An order issued by a judge, usually during court proceedings, prohibiting a property owner from a transferring the title while the lawsuit or case is proceeding. .

Writ of Execution - After a judgment has been issued against a property owner, the court may issue a writ of execution instructing the local authority to seize and sell the property at an judicial sale.

Write-Off - Expenses or deductions that can be used to lower a person's or entity's taxable income.

Yield - The net return on an investment. An investment's yield usually akes into account certain expenses. For example, a 1-year Treasury bill may pay guarantee a payment of $100 on a $1,000 bill--that's a 10% interest and yield. If the original owner sells this T-bill to another investor for $1,100, that new investor would be receiving a yield of only 9.0909% ($100/$1,100). [Note that mortgage rates are often tied to yields of Treasury notes. As these notes get more expensive, their yield and the corresponding mortgage rates go down.]

Yield Curve - In the securities market, the yield curve is the graphic representation of the different yields of short-term, mid- term and long-term U.S. Treasury notes. The 1-year T-Bill would have lower yields than the long-term 30-year T- Bonds. When a line is drawn from the yields of the 1-year T-Bill, through the medium-term notes, to the 30-year T-Bond's yield, the line is usually an ascending curve. In rare occasions, however, an inverted yield curve may arise.

Yield Spread Premium - The compensation brokers normally receive from the lender. This compensation, if any, is normally expressed as basis points and is based on the interest rate.

Zoning - The division of a city or county into areas (zones), specifying the uses of the land and building codes regulating each area. Zoning classifications vary by locale. See also related Variance and Covenant entries.

Zoning Amendment - A formal change to zoning regulation.

Zoning Board - The local committee or department responsible for reviewing and approving zoning appeals and requests.

ABOUT THE AUTHOR

William E Keeler has over eighteen years of experience in New York real estate as both a Salesperson and Broker in residential and commercial real estate rentals and sales. He was a member of the Long Island Multiple Listing Service, Long Island Board of Realtors, the New York State Association of Realtors and The National Association of Realtors. He studied real estate appraisal with the Columbia Society of Real Estate Appraisers. He was also a Certified Phase I Environmental Inspector with the National Environmental Association.

ADDITIONAL BOOKS BY WILLIAM E KEELER

Real Estate
Own It! For First Time Home Buyers
Own It! Home Buying Planner
Own It! Financial Planner
OWN IT! REAL ESTATE DICTIONARY